Human Resources Essentials

Employee Management & HR Planning Simplified

By: Dave Young

ALL RIGHTS RESERVED

No part of this book may be reproduced, stored in a retrieval system, or transmitted in any form or by any means, electronic, mechanical, photocopying, recording, scanning, or otherwise, without the prior written permission of the publisher.

Limit of Liability/Disclaimer of Warranty: the publisher and the author make no representations or warranties with respect to the accuracy or completeness of the contents of this work and specifically disclaim all warranties, including without limitation warranties of fitness for a particular purpose. No warranty may be created or extended by sales or promotional materials. The advice and strategies contained herein may not be suitable for every situation. This work is sold with the understanding that the publisher is not engaged in rendering medical, legal or other professional advice or services. If professional assistance is required, the services of a competent professional person should be sought. Neither the publisher nor the author shall be liable for damages arising herefrom. The fact that an individual, organization or website is referred to in this work as a citation and/or potential source of further information does not mean that the author or the publisher endorses the information the individuals, organization or website may provide or recommendations they/it may make. Further, readers should be aware that websites listed on this work may have changed or disappeared between when this work was written and when it is read.

Table of Contents

Introduction 1
Chapter 1: The Evolution of HR 3
    The Evolution of Employment 4
    The Rise of HR 7
    The Purpose of HR 8
    The Functions of HR 9
    The Trends in HR 16
    New Roles for HR Managers 19
    The Future of HR 24
Chapter 2: People, Resources, and Performance 27
    Performance Management and Development 28
    Effective Recruitment Strategies 31
    Employee Retention and Turnover Management 33
    Employee Development 36
    Succession Planning Implementation 41
    Employee Recognition 44
    Employee Satisfaction 47
Chapter 3: Managing Change and Developing HR Policies 51
    Change Management 51
    Restructuring and Downsizing 62
    Human Resource Planning Principles 64

Policies and Procedures 66

Pregnancy and Maternity Leave Policies 67

Employee Training and Development Plans 70

Workplace Flexibility Policies 79

Chapter 4: Linking Compensation to Company Strategy 82

Employee Benefits: An Overview of Major Programs 85

Combining base pay and incentives 88

Incentive plan design 92

Compensation budgeting 98

Bonus Plans Best Practices 104

Chapter 5: Internal Communications 110

Engaging Employees 113

Resolving Employee Issues 117

The Communication Process 120

Developing a Communications Strategy 126

Chapter 6: Mitigating Legal Risks in HR 130

Information sharing 130

Privacy, security, and confidentiality 133

Employment contracts and agreements 136

Compliance with laws and regulations 139

Employment terminations and layoffs 144

Hiring employees 146

Chapter 7: HR Systems and Technology 150

Achieving Results through Human Resource Systems . 151

Employee Relations Management Systems 156
Human Resource Information Systems 160
Application Tracking System 164
Learning and Development Systems 166
Enterprise Communication System 171
Conclusion 173

Introduction

Human Resource Management is an important part of any business, and it is perhaps more important for a small business than a large corporation. This is because human resource management in a small business is the entire structure of the company. The owners are often also the managers and the employees, therefore, all decisions made in human resource management must be made based on the best interests of the company.

Human resource management can be divided into two areas: employee management and HR planning. Employee management involves ensuring that everyone has the proper training, motivation, evaluation, and compensation to make them productive members of your team. HR planning involves deciding what kind of people you want to hire and then developing strategies to find them.

This book is designed for small business owners or managers who want to manage their employees in the most effective manner possible. It is also aimed at students who are interested in a career in human resource management.

This book will focus on the topics surrounding employee management and HR planning. After reading this book, you should be able to develop a plan for managing your employees to make them happy and productive. You will also be able to develop a strategy for recruiting and hiring new employees.

After reading this book, you will be able to:

- Understand how to manage employees to their fullest potential.
- Understand the ways to motivate your employees.
- Develop the best strategies for evaluating your employees.
- Determine the best compensation strategy for each employee.
- Develop the best strategies for hiring new employees.
- Understand the purpose and use of human resource planning tools.

With that, let's begin with a review of the basics of human resource management.

Chapter 1: The Evolution of HR

The ability of a company to grow and survive in the market is determined by its strategic planning. Strategic planning is the process of creating a long-term vision that will work toward making the company successful in the future. Unfortunately, not all companies have a proper strategy because they do not know where they want to be in 20 years. This is where human resource management comes in, and it can help an organization chart out its future growth path.

Human resource management is defined as a process of managing people within an organization. This is the process of hiring, training, developing, and terminating people. The human resource management department is responsible for creating a positive work environment for the employees where they can thrive and grow.

In today's date, the human resource management department is responsible for everything from hiring to staff development to managing performance. It also focuses on career planning and succession planning. The skillset of an HR professional must be such that it can adapt to any situation and any type of employee.

HR professionals are often required to be multi-taskers because they have many roles in an organization. The HR professional must not only handle all the responsibilities that come with being a manager but also give his/her best as a leader and coach. He/she must make sure that employees are motivated in every situation and learn from their mistakes to improve themselves and the company's financial standing.

HR is often misunderstood by many people because it has so many responsibilities on its plate. It is not just about managing employees but also about improving their productivity which can be done by bringing out their best through training programs.

If you want to become a successful HR manager, you must first understand where the position came from. The role of an HR manager has evolved over the years due to the changing needs of employees and organizations.

We will cover the evolution of HR through this chapter and try to understand how the HR department has evolved in the past few decades.

The Evolution of Employment

The first job that was created by humans was when they started farming. They employed people to work for them which would help them tend to the land and farm. As time passed, humans started moving to towns and cities where they had the opportunity to work with other people. As a result, they started employing people from different backgrounds like doctors, teachers, and other job roles. Even these employees were not permanent because they worked on temporary contracts. The employers would pay a set amount of money for every day that an employee worked, and after a certain amount of time, they would be terminated from their jobs. This is how the first employment contracts came into existence.

It was during this era that human resource management was born because there were employees who did not want to be treated as objects of employment and wanted greater recognition and respect. This led to unions being formed to protect the rights of workers and their families in case of any injustice or violation of human rights by employers or managers.

After World War II, many changes took place in the world which led to advanced technology being incorporated into workplaces. Manufacturing organizations were reduced significantly due to automation processes becoming more dominant than ever before - this led to higher unemployment rates. This is when the first employment laws came into being, and the role of human resource management in this era was to ensure that workers were protected, and their rights safeguarded.

Employment laws were introduced to protect employees from exploitation because they would often be paid low wages for long hours of work and forced to work in unsafe conditions. To ensure employers complied with these laws, human resource management professionals started working closely with government regulators and unions. HR managers also worked closely with the legal team to make sure that employees got paid what they were legally entitled to.

As time passed, organizations started becoming more sophisticated, which meant that instead of hiring one person for one job, organizations were hiring multiple people who had different skill sets. This led to the specialization of jobs and an enormous growth in HR departments due to higher demand for skilled professionals. People now work as specialists instead of generalists, which means that they have extensive knowledge about one particular area and have a varied skill set but they do not know everything about everything, as it was required earlier.

With time, companies also began focusing on their core competencies where they worked towards improving the strengths of their organization so that it could become better than its competitors in the field. The role of HR in this scenario is to find the best talent from within its organization and improve the company's performance. The HR department plays a key role in employee retention because it can identify whether the employees are performing well or not which also helps in improving employee retention.

As time passed, companies became more specialized, and with that came a need for specialization within an organization as well. This led to managers having to hire specialized skilled professionals, so that they could carry out complex tasks which were not possible before due to lack of expertise. This also led to specialization of HR professionals because there was a higher demand for professionals who could help organizations improve their workforce.

Another thing that happened during this period was the transformation of employment from being permanent to temporary which allowed companies to hire people on short-term contracts. This also resulted in many people quitting their jobs after working on these contracts because they could not find better positions outside and were forced back into unemployment. This was why temporary employment also gave rise to unemployment in the first place.

The Rise of HR

With temporary employment, a need for skilled professionals also arose. This is where the HR department came in because it could hire people on short-term contracts and then retain them by offering them better positions so that they would not quit their jobs.

With the rise of human resources came a demand for HR managers who could find talent from within the organization and develop it. It was also during this time that new HR skills started coming into existence. Before this, people were involved in HR without any skills or education - they just had good communication skills. This allowed them to deal with employees effectively. However, with the rise of human resources, professionals started going through extensive training courses to make sure that they were qualified enough for their job role. The complexity of these roles meant that professionals had to go through college or university to get trained in what is needed for their job role.

This is when professional associations like the Chartered Institute of Personnel & Development (CIPD) were formed which taught professionals how to become effective managers within an organization and effectively manage employees. Many people went on to become CIPD members because they wanted a standard qualification certificate from a recognized institute while working as an HR professional.

As more organizations hired HR professionals, they began focusing on training and developing their employees. This led to a change in the HR department over the years, where a lot of people started focusing on human resources rather than just managing them. It became a full-fledged department and started playing an important role in strategic planning and business decision making.

The Purpose of HR

We will try to understand the purpose of HR first, and then we will review how the purpose has evolved over the years.

The purpose of human resource management is to ensure that employees are happy at work and are productive in their jobs. In the long run, it is also responsible for creating great leaders who can take the company to greater heights. The HR department does not initiate any action but rather follows a set process and documents all actions that are taken.

Human resource management focuses on three things:

Human Capital

Human capital is the most valuable asset in an organization, and without it, no matter how much money you have, you can't survive in the market. The human resource department ensures that employees are happy and well-trained because they know that these people can take a company to great heights if they are motivated enough. They also ensure that employees perform up to their potential so that there is greater output from them which means more profits for the company. If there is low productivity, then there will be no extra money coming in for the organization which will lead to losses and ultimately bankruptcy of the company.

Culture

It is very important for an organization to have a good culture because it helps in creating a positive work environment. The HR department is responsible for creating a good culture where employees are happy and motivated at work. This can be done by getting the right people on board and keeping them engaged with the right compensation packages. It can also be done by training employees to be better leaders who can take the company forward with their wisdom and knowledge.

Succession Planning

Succession planning is an important aspect of human resource management because it helps an organization move towards the future without losing its values and vision. It ensures that everything runs smoothly, even when there is a change in leadership which is usually inevitable after a few years.

The Functions of HR

The human resource department is divided into several departments which are responsible for various tasks including recruitment, training, and other tasks. We will be looking into each of these departments one by one so that you can understand what each of them does and how they fit into the scheme of things in an organization. We will also discuss what makes them important for an organization's success or failure over time.

Recruitment Division

The recruitment division is responsible for finding potential candidates who are required to fill certain vacancies in an organization based on the requirements of the job. This division is responsible for creating a positive image of the company so that it attracts the right candidates who are interested in joining the company.

The recruitment department is usually headed by a manager who oversees recruitment activities. He/she is responsible for finding suitable candidates for open positions and hiring the right person for the job. The manager works in tandem with other departments like the Human Resource Development and Training to find suitable candidates for jobs.

The manager makes sure that all legal documents are signed before a candidate joins as an employee of an organization. He/she also makes sure that all employees are listed on payroll and given all necessary benefits like medical insurance, pension plans, and other crucial services.

The manager must make sure that there are no loopholes in the recruitment process, or else people can file lawsuits against an organization accusing them of discrimination or other illegal practices during recruitment activities. It is important to hire the right people because they will be representing your organization to potential clients and customers, so you must be very careful while conducting interviews or asking them any questions during their job interviews.

It is also important to ensure that employees get along well with each other, which means effective team building exercises need to be conducted every now and then. If the recruitment process is not done properly, then an organization can face a lot of problems in future because employees who have been hired might not be productive or even suitable for the job.

Human Resource Development

The human resource development department is responsible for training and educating employees so that they can handle the responsibilities of their jobs better. This department also has a hand in developing leaders who can take the company to greater heights in the long run.

The human resource department works with other departments like Human Resource Development (HRD) and Training to make sure that employees are trained and up-skilled, so that they can handle new technologies and deal with any crisis which might come up during their tenure at the company. Human Resource Development constitutes the framework for helping employees enhance their knowledge and abilities, thereby improving the performance of the firm. Additionally, they also focus on leadership development to make sure that there are no issues with succession planning, or other things that might come up.

The manager of this department is responsible for implementing all training programs which are designed by other departments like HRD and Training. He/she also keeps track of training activities and ensures that employees perform up to their potential after every training session.

This manager is also responsible for making sure that all employees receive proper training on a regular basis because new technologies are coming out every day, and if people don't keep themselves updated, they will not be able to perform efficiently in the long run.

Employee Relations

The employee relations department is responsible for dealing with the issues of employees on a day-to-day basis. This department is headed by a manager who looks at the grievances of employees and tries to solve them.

He/she also tries to resolve issues between two employees or departments so that there are no conflicts within the organization. He/she also deals with grievances of ex-employees who have left the organization and demands for unpaid wages, and other things they might have missed during their time there.

The manager must deal with all these issues efficiently because if people feel that their voice is not being heard, they will leave the company and look for better opportunities elsewhere, which can be detrimental to an organization's reputation among its clients and customers. He/she also must make sure that there are no clashes between management and employees because it can affect productivity in an organization in a negative way which will eventually lead to its failure in the market.

Employee Health Benefits

This department is responsible for handling health benefits provided by an organization like medical insurance, dental insurance, and other kinds of insurance packages. The manager of this department is responsible for going through all health benefit packages from insurance companies so that he/she can offer the best benefits at a reasonable price. He/she also must ensure that all benefits are offered to employees because that is one of the reasons why many people join an organization.

The manager must make sure that employees have access to all health benefits and get proper treatment in time of medical emergencies. This will keep employees happy and healthy, so that they can perform better at work. Health benefits are a major deciding factor for many candidates, and if an organization offers good health insurance, it is likely to attract the right candidates who might not be interested in working for another organization because of the lack of health benefits.

The manager must make sure that the company offers medical insurance with good coverage, and in case there are no such packages available, he/she will have to find out from other companies, so that employees can take benefit of them.

Employee Training

This department is responsible for the employees' training needs. Every organization needs employees who can perform their job well and there is no better way of doing so than through proper training.

Employees need to be trained to understand how their work fits with the larger picture and what role they play in it. They also need to be trained about the products that the company sells because they must sell them to customers and gain more business for the company.

Training is essential because a company's performance depends on how well employees perform when they are on the job, and if they do not know how to do their job properly, it will affect an organization's efficiency in a very negative way. The manager of this department must train new hires as soon as possible after their hiring so that they can start working right away.

He/she also must train all employees at regular intervals so that they stay updated with changes in technology, policies, and other possible changes. It is also important for employees to be trained about how customer service plays a crucial role for an organization's success and failure in the market because that will increase their motivation levels which will eventually help them perform better at work.

Compensation and Benefits

The compensation and benefits department has several responsibilities which include salary administration, compensation management, and benefits administration. Compensation and benefits play a crucial role in retaining employees because good pay will keep them happy at work, while bad pay will force them to look elsewhere for better opportunities.

Employees need to know how much their work is worth in the organization so that they can get motivated by it. A bad compensation plan will have a negative impact on an organization's performance because it will lead to employee dissatisfaction. This can lead to low motivation levels which usually results in poor performance at work.

The manager of this department has a responsibility towards his/her employees as well as the company because he/she must understand what his/her employees want and make sure that the company provides it. If the manager does not understand what employees want, then he/she will end up losing good workers which will affect the morale of the company.

Staffing and Labor Relations

This department is responsible for staffing issues and labor relations in an organization. It is responsible for making sure that there is a proper balance between the number of workers and their workload so that they can perform better at work.

The manager of this department must handle several problems like disputes between workers and management, absenteeism, staff turnover, and other issues. The staffing part of this department needs to keep track of every worker's performance so that the workers can be rewarded accordingly or terminated if their performance is bad.

This department is also responsible for handling labor relations in an organization because it needs to take care of legal matters related to labor laws. A poorly handled labor relations issue can lead to strikes and other legal problems which will affect an organization's performance in a very negative way.

Separation and Termination

The separation and termination divisions are responsible for handing out severance packages to employees who are being terminated. Employees who are getting fired often feel unhappy about it, and they will not contribute to the organization's development anymore.

It is the duty of this department to make sure that employees get compensated for their work at an appropriate time. A well-managed out-processing department will mean a happy employee who has a positive attitude towards his/her work, which will help the organization in the long run.

The Trends in HR

The Human Resource Management department is one of the most important departments in any organization. It has evolved from being the personnel department to a strategic unit that can bring in more value to an organization. It is now treated as a business partner and sometimes, it is even more valued than the CEO. This change in perception is due to the changing needs of employees and organizations.

Today, HR is a strategic department that is responsible for many areas of an organization. It must deal with everything from hiring to firing and everything in between. To understand the evolution of HR, we need to look at the trends in HR and how they affect business today.

The most important trend in HR is the changing nature of work. The role of an employee has changed since the industrial revolution took place. Today, people are not just expected to come to work and leave at a certain time. They are also expected to be available through their mobile devices at all times and be connected anywhere in the world via the internet.

People are also becoming more aware of their rights as employees and want fair treatment, too. This has forced companies to change their policies and treat employees with respect which was not common earlier. Organizational culture has also evolved over time from being competitive towards a more collaborative approach. This is evident from the way employees interact with each other today.

The need for efficiency across departments has improved as well because businesses need faster results today than ever before due to market competition. This need for efficiency has led people towards outsourcing some jobs which has been made possible by technology advancements in communication like Skype, WhatsApp, and other online communication services.

The increased emphasis on business ethics and corporate governance has made a huge impact on the way organizations function. To comply with laws and maintain transparency, HR departments have been given more responsibility. This is evident from the role of an HR manager today.

Technology has also played a huge role in improving the efficiency of HR. This revolution began with the advent of the computer and continues today through advanced software like HR Software, which has changed the way organizations will function.

HR technologies have not only improved efficiency but also brought a lot of innovation. HR professionals can now use cloud-based software to streamline their work and simplify their tasks.

This revolution in technology has allowed people to move away from paper-based processes and adopt more digital platforms that make their work a lot easier. This change is so significant that it has also led to an increase in the number of jobs that require digital skills than hard skills. This will continue to grow as technology evolves and brings more innovations into our lives.

The increased popularity of outsourcing has also played a role in changing the roles of HR professionals because they are now responsible for managing these outsourced workers as well. The trend is so strong that companies are finding it difficult to find enough skilled employees themselves which is why they are forced to outsource some of their work or hire contractors instead of full-time employees.

The changing nature of work has forced companies to become more innovative which is evident from how HR departments came into existence in the first place. HR professionals are often required to deal with a variety of tasks and responsibilities.

Hiring and firing employees is the most important role of an HR manager because it has a huge impact on the company's financial turnover. The hiring process is often handled by HR professionals because they are responsible for creating a positive work environment for employees. They do this by following a set of rules that make sure that the company hires the right employee according to their needs.

Creating an efficient onboarding process is also one of the most important roles of an HR professional because it can have a huge impact on employee productivity. It is because of this reason that many companies hire professional onboarding experts to train their employees and bring them up to speed in very little time.

HR professionals also must make sure that they are complying with all applicable laws concerning employment and workplace harassment, and other such problems. It is through these laws that organizations have become more transparent and fairer toward their employees.

New Roles for HR Managers

Before the role of an HR manager was introduced, there were already many departments that were responsible for the employee's well-being. These departments included the human resource department, personnel department and labor relations department.

In today's date, human resource management is a separate function that is responsible for employee management and staff development.

The various roles of an HR professional are explained below:

Compliance and Legislation Roles

The role of an HR professional has evolved over the years due to changing employment laws. The staff turnover has dropped considerably because employees now have more rights than they did in the past.

Many companies are concerned about staying compliant with all laws because it can lead to heavy fines if they do not adhere to them. As an HR professional, you will be required to keep your company updated with all new legislations and make sure that all employees stay aware about their rights as well. You will also be required to handle employee grievances regarding compliance issues.

Employee Engagement Role

Another important role of an HR professional is ensuring that employees are engaged throughout their time in the organization. If employees are not engaged at work, they will leave the company no matter how much compensation you offer them. Employee engagement is an important part of human resource management and it should be handled by someone with leadership skills.

The employee engagement role is often confused with the performance management role which focuses on identifying and developing high potential employees. To keep your employees engaged, you must make sure that they are motivated about their work and that they work towards achieving company goals.

Another factor that affects employee engagement is the pay system that you offer to your employees. If a company does not offer good pay, it will have trouble retaining its best employees because they can easily find another job elsewhere where they can get better pay packages. Here, we will discuss the various compensation plans offered by companies and how effective they are in retaining talent.

Training Role

An HR professional is responsible for making sure that his/her team members are trained properly before they enter the workforce. Top organizations train their employees for up to six months before they start working with them.

This training period is used to teach new hires about the organization's culture, mission statement, and other core values of the company. Training programs help new hires become productive and useful for the organization right away instead of taking a long time to learn their job roles and responsibilities. Many companies invest a lot of money in training because they understand that a trained employee is more valuable than an untrained one.

However, most companies have a short training period for new employees because they cannot afford to invest so much time and money into them when there is always the risk of them quitting early on. With the rapidly changing environment, it is important to update your training programs so that they are relevant to the market. A good HR professional should be able to find out which topics are outdated and should be replaced with new topics.

Employee Wellness Role

An HR professional must also focus on employee wellness and ensure that employees take care of themselves. This includes managing their health insurance and making sure that they do not get sick or injured at work.

It also includes providing resources like access to medical facilities, and encouraging healthy lifestyles. The role of an HR professional is not only limited to employee management but also extends towards their wellbeing. An employee who gets sick due to overwork will only work slower which will negatively impact the company's productivity levels.

The health of employees should always be taken care of by an HR professional because he/she understands that a healthy workforce can contribute more to the organization's success than an unhealthy one.

Performance Management Role

This role is responsible for making sure that employees work towards achieving company goals. It is the responsibility of an HR professional to identify the best employees in the organization and assign them to high-level positions.

This will motivate them to perform well which will only lead to a positive effect on the overall performance of the company. If an employee does not deliver what is expected of him/her, it is the responsibility of an HR professional to take corrective measures and make sure that he/she improves his/her performance immediately.

Once an employee understands his/her weaknesses, he/she can work on improving them with a coach or mentor. If they do not improve, it is up to the HR professional to terminate their contracts or transfer their roles elsewhere to reduce the negative impact on their current team members.

The performance management role focuses more on identifying high potential employees and making them successful. To spot high potential employees, you need to understand what your competitors are doing well and make sure that your organization has an edge over theirs by highlighting unique strengths in your HR programs.

For example, if you have excellent training programs for new hires, you can attract better talent than those who do not offer training programs at all.

The performance management role is also responsible for managing employee's career paths and making sure that they are on the right track. Managers often get carried away with employee retention because they do not want to lose their top performers. However, they should realize that if an employee has been performing well for a long time, it is only logical to transfer them to another department where they can grow further.

This will help them avoid stagnation and gain valuable skill sets which can make them even better employees in the future.

HR Analytics Roles

The main goal of having an HR analytics department is to achieve a high level of productivity and improve the overall performance of the company. These departments are responsible for creating metrics and reporting tools that will help managers identify areas that need improvement through analyzing data. For example, if you have multiple locations or departments in your organization, you can use reports and analytics tools to track performance across all locations. This will let you understand which departments are performing well while others need improvement. It is the responsibility of an HR professional to make sure that data is collected through various sources like surveys, and other methods before sending it over to the HR analytics team. With correct data and reporting tools, you can make better decisions about your company's performance and make improvements.

The performance of your company's HR department is also dependent on the quality of data that you collect. If you are not tracking the right information through the right methods, you cannot use analytics to make informed decisions which will only lead to poor decision making.

The HR analytics team should be focusing on gathering data that is relevant to employee management and staff development because it can help managers understand their teams better. For example, if a manager knows his/her team's strengths and weaknesses, he/she can develop an effective employee retention strategy by reducing stress points in their work.

The Future of HR

The future of HR is going to be very bright. The HR department has evolved tremendously in the past few decades, and it has become a profit center for many organizations. This has led to the growth of people analytics, and the HR professionals are no longer dependent on gut feeling or instinct when making decisions.

The HR professionals have access to large amounts of data that they can use to predict future problems. They can come up with solutions before problems arise and save a lot of money by avoiding expensive mistakes.

The future of HR is filled with technological advancements that will make the job easier for both companies and employees. Here are some predictions on how human resources will grow in the next few decades:

We will see more use of artificial intelligence & predictive analytics

HR managers will be able to use software like Big Data that helps them predict which candidate will be a good fit for an open position. This kind of software can also help predict which employees are likely to leave or get fired so that corrective measures can be taken in time. The cost savings from using these tools would save millions for most companies around the world.

There will be less focus on hiring

Although hiring is one of the most important responsibilities of HR professionals, it will become less of a focus as organizations start using predictive analytics. The HR professionals will be able to predict which candidate is likely to be successful and hire them before the position becomes open. This would free up HR managers to concentrate on other key tasks such as employee development & retention.

The employment contract will go away

As organizations start using predictive analytics, there will be no need for contracts because the employees would not quit without a reason. The HR managers can rely on the data to determine whether an employee is likely to leave and take corrective measures before they become an issue. This would save millions in legal fees and help an organization remain cost-competitive in the market.

The role of HR manager will evolve into a strategic role

Presently, the role of an HR manager has evolved from managing employees into managing an entire department. Unfortunately, this evolution has led to many problems with some HR managers taking on too much responsibility. In the future, it is expected that the role of an HR manager will evolve into a strategic role where only high-level decisions are made by him/her instead of participating in every process like hiring or firing. This will free up a lot of time for HR professionals.

The HR professionals will be able to have a larger impact on the business

Today, the HR professionals are often perceived as being middle-men and not having much of an impact on the business. This perception is not true because they can have a huge impact by improving employee productivity. In the future, it is expected that HR professionals will be able to have a larger impact on business growth.

In today's world, we can see how human resources has evolved into different roles like leadership and development. It has become an important part of most organizations because they need to focus on employee engagement and retention if they want to reduce costs and improve their overall profits. This evolution has also led to advancements in technology which allow organizations to get more out of their employees and achieve higher levels of productivity. It is expected that this trend will continue in the future, and there will be more changes in how organizations manage their employees.

Chapter 2: People, Resources, and Performance

In any business, people are the most important resource. They need to be well trained with consistent performance appraisal and rewards for good performance. Without them, a business cannot produce the products or render the services that it is set up to offer.

HR planning is simply about taking care of people in all aspects of their professional and personal lives so that they remain productive for the company. It could be as simple as helping them to hire a trustworthy nanny for their children. It could also be giving them some training to help them get better at their jobs or making the workplace more conducive to good health and productivity.

HR planning can also entail offering career tracks for people in different fields, so that they can grow within the company. It can also mean helping them find new avenues for their work when they are not happy with what they are currently doing at work.

The HR function is not just about people management at work, it is about making sure that the human resource of a company is fit and healthy so that it can deliver good results for the business and carry on with its operations smoothly. It means getting good services from an Employee Assistance Program (EAP), ensuring that employees do not get into substance abuse, addiction or other forms of self-destructive behavior which may impair their ability to work or create a liability for the company if they are involved in an accident on company time or at some event sponsored by the business.

It also means looking after employees who have special needs due to illness or disability and training staff in how to deal with these employees in such a way that it does not seem like special treatment.

In this chapter, we are going to look at the different aspects of human resources planning on people, resources, and performance, and how they contribute to the overall success of a business. We will also look at some of the specific aspects to each function of human resource management.

Performance Management and Development

Performance management is handled by the human resources department, which is responsible for performance appraisal of employees and ensuring that they are rewarded for good work. Performance management also largely deals with performance development.

Performance development is a system which helps an employee to learn to do his/her job better or acquire new skills so that he/she can take on more responsibilities and deliver better results. It is usually conducted by an experienced expert in the field. It is generally given to employees who have been with the company for a few years and have demonstrated good performance at work but who are not often promoted into higher positions in the company.

Performance appraisal may be done periodically or on a continuous basis. If it is done on a continuous basis, then the employee must work with his/her supervisor to determine what he/she needs to improve and how best he/she can achieve the goals set by the company. It could be as simple as improving customer service skills or learning a new software application so that more work can be outsourced.

Companies generally use a standard method for performance appraisal, but employees are given ample opportunity to discuss their appraisals and ask questions if they feel that something is wrong. In fact, most companies have formal grievance redressal mechanisms, where employees can submit complaints about unfair appraisals or other forms of harassment at work. It is only after these grievances have been addressed that they should go ahead and file for compensation if necessary.

An employee who has not had proper performance appraisal or development may not get promoted, or he/she might not be seen as a good candidate for a promotion. Also, in some cases, an employee may not get a raise if he/she has not improved his/her performance in the past few years. If the employee is under-performing and does not do anything to address this, then the company will have no choice but to let him/her go.

The most important thing for HR to understand about performance development is that training employees is not just about making them work faster and better in their current jobs. It is also about ensuring that they are ready for their next career move within the company. This means that they should be given the skills that they need to take on more responsibility, as well as any additional training needed to get them ready for higher positions in the company.

What should HR do regarding Performance Development?

The HR department is responsible for ensuring that employees are adequately trained to do their jobs and to make sure that they are given proper attention during performance review. They should also ensure that employees have enough time to perform their jobs well and get the required feedback from their supervisors. The HR department should be able to give them the training they need, whether it is in-house or external.

What are some of the common ways of Performance Development?

There are various ways of conducting performance development, and companies should find out which one suits them best. Some of these include:

1) Formal classroom training – This is usually conducted by a certified expert who can train employees in a particular skill or knowledge area. It involves lectures, group discussions and hands-on training to ensure that employees can apply what they have learned from the course at work. It can be on-site, but if it is too time consuming, it can also be conducted online or even through distance learning methods like e-learning or audio/visual learning modules.

2) On-the-job training – This is done by letting an employee shadow another employee who has been trained in this skill or knowledge area. This is usually done by placing the employee with an experienced senior employee who can give him/her tips on how to do the job better. It can also be done by allowing the employee to use tools or equipment which are new to him/her, but which he/she will be expected to use once

he/she becomes more familiar with the job and has learned how to operate them properly.

3) In-house training – This is conducted by allowing employees to use a part of their working hours to attend training classes conducted in-house, usually by someone who has been trained in this skill or knowledge area. It involves lectures, group discussions and hands-on training so that employees can apply what they have learned from the course at work.

4) E-learning - This means delivering training information through online courses and other computer-based tools for learning purposes. It allows for greater flexibility in terms of time and location of learning, but it may not be as interactive as other methods of training.

Effective Recruitment Strategies

There are numerous people involved in the recruitment process for a business from the people who advertise jobs to the person who interviews and selects the candidate. Here are some of the aspects of recruitment that need to be considered:

Advertising:

The first aspect is advertising. The aim is to attract candidates with the right qualifications and experience while not attracting unsuitable candidates who will only waste time and resources. This can be done by using appropriate keywords in the advertisement, such as "Fresh graduates welcome," or "Mature applicants only." The advertisement should also state clearly what job applicants can expect, such as a six-month contract or traineeship with opportunity for permanent employment. A good advertisement should give enough information about the job together with details of how to apply for it.

Employer Branding:

An employer's reputation is important when it comes to hiring employees because they will either be known for providing good work conditions or they will have an image associated with them that will turn off potential employees. Good employer branding can help attract more potential employees and reduce cost as well as turn-over time because new hires do not need as much training to become productive workers.

Search Engine Optimization:

One of the most important aspects of recruitment is search engine optimization, or SEO as businesses are more commonly referring to it today. This is simply about getting the right keywords in the advertisement so that it will appear when someone searches for a candidate with these qualifications.

Social Media:

Today, social media plays a very important role in the recruitment process because people tend to share their experiences about companies through social media sites. This can be used to your advantage by making sure that you have a good reputation on social media sites. You can do this by making sure that you respond quickly to any queries, complaints or suggestions made on social media. You can also post photos of your candidates and other employees to show what a pleasant workplace it is on your Facebook page or Twitter account.

Employee Retention and Turnover Management

The most important part of human resource planning is ensuring that the people in a company are well trained, and that they are properly motivated to do their jobs and stay with the company. This requires training, supervision, and even active intervention in personal lives where necessary.

Employee retention is one of the biggest challenges facing any business today, particularly in such industries as manufacturing and retail trade. To compete successfully with other companies offering similar products or services, customer service becomes extremely important. If a customer buys from one company because he has a good experience with the sales force or because she likes the way the people at checkout are attentive to her needs, they may not shop anywhere else.

This means that companies need to train their sales force to be friendly and knowledgeable about their products. They also need to set up systems for customer feedback so that they can respond quickly to complaints or concerns by customers and make them feel like they are being well taken care of. They also need good systems for quality control so that defective products do not get shipped out to customers who then complain about them or return them for refunds.

On the other hand, if a customer has a bad experience at checkout because an employee was rude or spent more time playing around with his friends, he/she may not come back. This is where employee retention becomes very important. The company needs to train its employees to be efficient and helpful. It also needs to set up a system of regular performance reviews so that it can reward good performance and weed out the troublemakers.

Training employees and providing them with opportunities for advancement within the company are very important for the future growth and success of any business. Retaining experienced staff is also important, since most new hires need time to get up to speed on how things work in an organization, develop professional relationships with peers and supervisors, and build up their skills so that they can be effective at what they do.

Another aspect of employee retention is making sure that people do not leave because they are unhappy about something at work or because they got demoted or fired unfairly. While this may not necessarily have a direct impact on the company's profits, it can hurt morale and affect productivity, particularly if one or two bad apples cause a lot of trouble for everyone else.

It can also have a negative impact on the company's reputation because disgruntled employees are likely to talk about their experience and may even try to start a union in their workplace. This can be very disruptive. The company could lose its competitive edge in the marketplace, resulting in lower profits and revenues.

Employee turnover is therefore another area where human resource planning is important for business success, because companies need to make sure that they are retaining good people and finding new ones when necessary. They need to make sure that they have enough people working for them so that they do not get caught short without enough suppliers or workers when there is an unexpected increase in demand for their products or services.

There are several aspects of employee retention which should be taken into consideration by human resource managers. They include:

Employee Attraction

The first thing that human resource managers need to do is to find out how to attract the best employees for their company. They may have to go beyond the local labor market to get them and may even have to think about relocating to a place where they can find the kind of employees they want.

They can also think about ways to make their company more attractive. This could mean offering better benefits, improved working conditions or training opportunities for workers who want them. It could also mean improving workplace safety and security so that staff do not feel threatened by violent or abusive customers, or they do not feel like they are risking personal safety every time they go out on a sales call.

Employee Retention

The next thing that HR managers need to do is look at ways in which their company can retain its employees for longer periods of time. They need to make sure that there is an adequate system for rewarding good performance and taking care of problem employees before they cause too much trouble for everyone else. They also need a system in place for helping unhappy employees find new jobs within the company.

Employee Turnover

The third thing that HR managers should look at is ways to control employee turnover, particularly in such industries as retail and manufacturing where the number of workers fluctuates according to the season. They need to make sure that there are enough workers always available and that they are properly trained so that they can provide good customer service. They also need to set up a system for helping workers find new jobs when they leave the company, hopefully before they quit or get fired.

Retraining Programs

The fourth thing that human resource managers need to consider is retraining programs for employees who are not able to keep up with changes in their industry or their particular job functions. They need to make sure that such programs are available for people who want them and do not feel threatened by them. They also need to make sure that these programs will be effective in helping people keep up with the changes being made by their company to stay competitive.

Employee Development

Employee development consists of all the training programs that are designed to help employees to develop and grow with the company. It may be training in new skills, acquiring additional knowledge, or improving performance in a specific field.

Training should be a continuous process in any organization. It is necessary to impart skills and knowledge to all employees, at all levels, so they can perform their jobs better. It is also important for them to understand the business and its objectives for them to work more effectively.

When you hire someone for your company, you need to find out what kind of training they have had and what they are used to doing at work. Some people need more training than others because they have not been trained previously or because their previous employers did not provide them with training opportunities. These people usually require additional support from an orientation program or some other form of leadership training. This will help them get up to speed as quickly as possible with the company's policies and procedures as well as its overall goals and objectives.

If you have well-trained staff from the start, it will save you time and money over time on maintenance training because they will be able to perform their jobs better from day one, and that is often half the battle in any career.

Building a sense of team spirit and camaraderie among employees is also important so they do not work like a bunch of individuals. They will work much better as a team if they can feel that they are on the same page and pulling in the same direction. Effective training creates an environment where employees feel like they are all working towards the same goal, so they do not have to be reminded about it all the time. It does not have to be constantly repeated to them because they already know what must be done to achieve that goal. This makes them more productive and efficient at their jobs because there is no need for so much supervision and leading from above since they are already aware of what needs to be done.

For your training program to be effective, it needs to have clear objectives and goals which people understand and want to achieve. Training needs to be relevant both to your company's overall goals as well as its employees' personal objectives. The objectives should be achievable within a certain time frame, so people can see where they stand at each stage of their development plan.

A good training program will also include some form of informal or formal evaluation during or after training to see how well the people were able to absorb the training and if or when they are ready to move on to the next level of training. This is also a good time to give feedback about the effectiveness of the training and how it can be improved or changed in future.

Training programs should be developed with your employees' input, if possible, so that they know what skills they need for their jobs and feel like they are a part of developing their own skill set. They will work more productively if they feel that their participation in developing this is important for them personally as well as for their company. It shows them that you are serious about your commitment towards improving your employees' performance as well as maintaining company growth.

For employees to do their jobs effectively, they need specific tools and equipment for their specific position. They may not be able to do their jobs if they do not have the appropriate tools and equipment at hand. For them to continue doing their jobs, you need to provide them with those tools and equipment.

In a manufacturing company, your employees may need specific hand or power tools for their work. They may also need protective gear, so they are safe from hazards such as heat, cold, or noise while they are working. As an employer, you need to make sure that they have these things available for them at work before you expect them to perform their jobs effectively.

In an office environment, some of the tools and equipment for the employees include computers, software programs, telephones, and other means of communication. This is especially important for people who work in sales because they might have to deal with customers over the telephone or send out emails all day long to sell products or services. If you expect these people to sell effectively over the phone or via email or social media websites such as Facebook or Twitter, then you need to make sure that they can communicate well with others through these media platforms without having to worry about technical problems or any other issues that may interfere with their work.

If your employees often travel to perform their jobs, you need to make sure that they have the appropriate transportation for their work. If they need to go from place to place to perform their jobs, you need to provide them with a vehicle so that they can get around easily without having to worry about public transportation issues such as schedules, delays and other factors. This may distract them from doing their jobs effectively. In some cases, this could be a company car or a lease vehicle which you control and pay for. In other cases, it is a privately owned vehicle that you reimburse or reimburse for mileage.

Sometimes, people who work in sales or are in a field where they have to deal with the public frequently will need specific personal protective devices such as security badges and identification cards so that they are identified as company representatives. This is primarily a concern for people who are not necessarily associated with the company all the time but who have special access rights because of their job functions.

The tools and equipment needed by your employees will depend on what kind of business you run and what kind of products you sell or services you offer. It is important to define specifically what your employees need, so you can provide them with adequate tools and equipment for their jobs.

The Human Resource Manager needs to know what kind of training is required by the company's staff and how it can be provided in a way that meets the company's objectives and the employee's personal objectives.

Providing A Full Range of Training and Development Services

The HR manager will also need to work with the training department to make sure that they are able to provide the full range of training and development services required by employees at all levels of their career. It is important that employees have a clear view of their career plans and how they can move up within the company, so they know where to focus their efforts.

There will also be times when an employee has different goals from those of the company or when an employee is not performing well or is not a good fit with the culture of the organization. In these cases, it may require some counseling or coaching to help them understand how their goals can be adjusted to align more closely with those of the organization.

In some situations, people may not be able to continue working with your organization because of personal issues which need to be addressed outside work. These may be problems with drug abuse or alcohol abuse which prevent people from performing their jobs in a professional manner. They may also have certain family or health issues which prevent them from doing their work well. In these cases, the HR manager will need to find a solution which makes the employee happy and does not affect the performance of the department.

Making Programs Relevant

Training and development are important parts of any organization, but can only be effective if relevant to what people do in their jobs, if they understand how it benefits them, and if they have the willingness to learn what they need to know or do what their job requires of them.

The HR manager is responsible for making sure that people are trained and developed effectively so that they can perform their jobs well and improve as people to get more out of life. It also needs to make sure that there are no problems with training programs which cause a disruption to operations or create resentment among staff members.

Succession Planning Implementation

Succession planning is one of the main aspects of human resources planning. It is about ensuring that there are people in place who can take over when a person leaves the company. It is also about setting up processes and procedures which make it easier to handover responsibilities or tasks from one person to another.

Performance Appraisals

One of the main tools used for succession planning is the performance appraisal, which gives the supervisors an opportunity to give feedback on what a person has been doing and how it contributes to the operation of the company. The next step would be to look at training opportunities for this person, so that they can be better prepared to take on added responsibilities if, for example, there are some people who go on long term leave or even leave for good.

Performance appraisal is also a good tool to use when it comes to awarding promotions within an organization. The supervisor can not only look at how this employee has performed in their current job but also see how they perform in any additional responsibilities that they may have taken on as well as what kind of training they may have undergone as part of their professional development within the company. This will help them get a clearer picture of who has been doing well and who needs some help or development before being considered for promotion.

Peer Feedback

Another way of using performance appraisal is to get feedback from people who interact with the employee on a regular basis, on how well they perform their duties and how well they interact with other people in the workplace. This is also useful when it comes to determining whether or not a person has what it takes to be promoted or even for someone new to be hired into the position.

Comparing Career Tracks

One of the main ways that HR departments can help with succession planning is by looking at career tracks for different positions within the company and developing a plan which will guide employees in their development within an organization. This will not only help them prepare for promotions but also allow them to see what kind of training they can pursue as part of their development within an organization, so they can better prepare themselves for any future opportunities that may come up in the company.

Career tracks are also helpful when it comes to dealing with employees who may feel trapped or unhappy with where they are at present in their careers and want to move elsewhere in the company. As part of this process, HR departments need to look at how others have fared when trying out other tasks or moving around different departments and try to find patterns which will help these people to plan out a career path for themselves within the company.

This can also help them to find new opportunities if they feel that they have been doing the same thing for too long and want a change. It will also help them decide whether or not they are going to be able to handle the responsibilities of this new position and how it will affect their performance in their current position.

Planning for Retirements

Another aspect of succession planning is planning for retirements. This means that HR departments need to not only find out when employees are going to be retiring but also look at how this can affect operations within the company and what kind of training people may need if there is a mid-term replacement or if there is a sudden departure which requires immediate action by another person in that position. They will need to look at what kind of gaps this may create in other parts of the company as well as how it might affect the work assignments of other people who report into that position.

The succession planning process should be ongoing, meaning that HR departments should have a list of people who can take over certain positions when an employee leaves for any reason, whether it is retirement, promotion or otherwise. This list should contain details on who these people are, what kind of training they have received and what kind of experience they have so that the department can look at the next steps to take when an employee leaves or plans to leave.

Employee Recognition

Employee recognition is one of the most important aspects of human resource planning. It is not costly and is also a very effective way of keeping employees happy and productive. There are many ways of recognizing employees, and here are some of the ways it can be done:

Cards, Emails, Letters, & Gifts

You could send a personally signed card or a notice to an employee expressing your appreciation for his or her work and efforts. Make sure that you keep your letters short and sweet. You do not want to come off as patronizing or sycophantic, but you should also not make your note sound too impersonal. You could also send an email to the employee thanking him or her for his hard work and efforts. Gifts are another great way of appreciating an employee, but remember to stay within your budget. Do not give any gift which is at all extravagant.

In addition, you could thank an employee by writing a short article about him or her which can be published in the company newsletter. You could also mention the names of people who have performed well and their achievements. This will serve as a motivation for those employees who are not getting recognition for their hard work.

Finally, you could send a personal gift to an employee on his or her birthday or on some other special occasion like Diwali or Christmas. This will surely make your employee feel more appreciated and valued by the company, and he or she will also feel more motivated to work harder for you.

For example, you could send a birthday present to an employee who has been with you for a long time. You could also send a gift on Diwali to an employee who has performed well, or someone who is having a tough time in his or her personal life.

In-House Events

In-house events are also another way of showing your employees that you appreciate their hard work and efforts. One such event could be a company picnic, either on an annual or quarterly basis, where everyone comes together and spends time together as colleagues and as friends. Ideally, it can be planned during holidays so that every employee is able to attend. You could make an announcement in advance so that the employees know when it is coming up. There are several ways in which this can be organized, but these things should not cost the company too much money. You should avoid spending too much on these events, because it will end up being counterproductive to your cause of encouraging good human resource management practices.

In addition, you could organize a yearly party for the employees, like a Diwali celebration, where they can all gather and have a good time. This would be good for morale, and it will also give the employees an opportunity to see each other in a different light. They will not be working while they are at the party, so they will also be able to relax with their colleagues and friends.

It is also best if you limit the number of guests per employee so that everyone gets value for money, since you will be charging them for their food and entertainment. You could get sponsorships from local businesses for this kind of event, but make sure that you do not offend anyone in your network by asking them to sponsor such an event, because they may feel offended at being approached in such a way. If you are going ahead with an in-house company event or picnic, make sure that you have everything planned out well in advance.

Some companies do not like the idea of having a company picnic because it is another way of eating into the company profits. However, to keep your employees happy, you may occasionally want to organize such an event. It will also be good for morale if you do this for your employees, and they will feel more appreciated and valued by the company. You could use these events as a form of recognition and reward for employees who have worked hard on some project or initiative.

Celebrations

If there is some milestone that has been achieved by the company as a whole or by one of your employees, then you should celebrate it. You could organize a small party to mark this occasion or get together for lunch or dinner at some restaurant outside the office premises if there is a particular reason behind this celebration event. This would once again show your employees that you appreciate them and their efforts, and it will motivate them to work harder in the future and be more productive at work. It will also be good for employee morale, since everyone likes to feel appreciated when he or she does something good, especially if it has been noticed by his or her boss.

Another milestone you could celebrate is the anniversary of your company. This is a good opportunity to give small tokens of appreciation to your employees and acknowledge their hard work and efforts over the years.

You could also just celebrate with a good meal at a restaurant or even with some cake, so your employees feel appreciated. When you are sincere in your appreciation, you will be able to motivate them to work harder for you.

Employee Satisfaction

Improving employee satisfaction is one of the key aspects of human resource management. This can be done by making sure that the workplace is safe and conducive to work. It can be done by increasing wages, providing good benefits like health insurance, retirement, or pension plans, and making sure that people have a say in how they are managed. It can also be done by giving people more responsibility and challenging them to perform better at their jobs.

Employee satisfaction is also increased by providing a clean and comfortable work environment. This includes providing sanitary facilities, furniture, air conditioning and heating, as well as providing lunchroom facilities.

It is also important to provide proper lighting and ventilation for employees to work effectively. For people who must work outside in the field, it is important to provide them with protective clothing and gear as well as refreshments.

Employee satisfaction can also be increased by increasing job security and providing greater opportunities for promotion. Employers can do this by keeping an eye on the performance of employees and giving them the opportunity to grow in their careers. It is a good idea to train employees in new skills and give them opportunities to work in different areas of the company.

Employee satisfaction is also increased by giving positive recognition to employees who have done well at their jobs. This can be done by praising good performance, giving rewards or bonuses, or sending employees on company outings or making them part of team activities.

Finally, employee satisfaction can be increased by encouraging employees to contribute ideas for improving the workplace or the company. Employees are more likely to remain loyal if they feel they have a say in how things are done in their workplace.

The best way to measure employee satisfaction is by using employee surveys.

How to conduct employee surveys

Employee surveys are usually done by the human resource department. When conducting an employee survey, it is important to keep the survey anonymous. This means that employees should not be able to recognize their name on the survey form. Also, employees should not be asked for their name or any other personal information.

Employers and Management members[1] can conduct employee surveys in several different ways. They can hold focus groups and ask employees questions one-on-one or in groups. They can also conduct telephone interviews, send out an email questionnaire or hold a company meeting to conduct an open forum discussion about employee satisfaction issues.

When conducting an employee survey, it is important to provide a list of questions for employees to answer and provide them with space for writing comments and suggestions. It is important that the questions are clearly written, so employees understand what they are being asked and why they are being asked these questions. It is also important to ensure that there is no bias in the questions asked, so responses reflect true feelings about work conditions rather than how employees feel they should answer.

---

[1] Reference for employee survey available from https://www.questionpro.com/blog/employee-survey/

A good way of ensuring that respondents give honest answers is by asking them hypotheticals rather than specific questions like: "Do you like working here?". For instance, they can be asked questions like: "How would you feel if the work hours were altered?" or "What changes would you like to see in order to improve the quality of the workplace?" It is also good to ask what employees would like to see changed in their workplace.

The results of the survey should be analyzed, and the findings should be presented to the company. Employers can use this information to make changes and improvements in the workplace.

Chapter 3: Managing Change and Developing HR Policies

This chapter will look at the process of changing management within a business from the perspective of the Human Resources function. It will examine the reasons for change within an organization, and why it is so important to have a change management process. It will also look at how HR can help to facilitate and manage change and help prevent resistance to it.

The chapter will then go on to examine some of the main reasons why people resist and oppose change, and how an organization can best manage this resistance, so that it does not affect performance, but ends up helping to improve performance.

Finally, we will look at policy development in organizations with particular emphasis upon HR policies. We will examine what is meant by policy development in an organization, why policies are needed within an organization and why they are important for both employees and employers. We will then look at some of the key considerations that need to be made when developing HR policies in an organization.

Change Management

Change is a constant activity within an organization. It is never stagnant and remains dynamic- changing and adapting to new conditions, new challenges, and new opportunities. The fact that an organization changes over time does not mean that it necessarily has a change management process in place.

However, this is usually the case, as most organizations wish to manage change effectively to maximize the benefits of it. It is not just the level of change that needs to be managed within an organization; it also needs to be managed effectively and efficiently. If change management is not carried out effectively, then it can have a negative impact on both productivity and performance.

The main reasons for change within an organization are:

Restructuring to increase efficiency and performance

The re-structure of any business will lead to the change in work location of employees, amalgamation of departments and addition/deletion of positions. This is not an easy task, as employees must be informed properly and re-trained, and some others must be released. These are very delicate processes which can cause a lot of problems if not handled with proper care.

Re-structuring can be a long process, and it is very important to ensure that employees are kept updated about the changes. The following steps will help in restructuring an organization:

Launching a new structure will require the following steps:

Inform employees about the changes which are to be implemented along with a proper communication plan.

Prepare a detailed plan of action with timelines for each stage of the restructure (such as informing employees, training, placement and so on). This will help in monitoring and keeping track of the progress made.

It is important to set up a clear chain of command so there are no problems in communication, and decisions are taken smoothly. This will also help in reducing confusion among employees about who they should report to and who they can turn to if any issues arise regarding their work or other issues related to their department.

A clear chain of command can also help when you want to implement new processes, as it will be easier for people to understand how they should be working under the new structure without any confusion or ambiguity arising out of it. They should know who is responsible for what and whom they should approach if there is any issue which needs to be solved.

You can also set up a task force of employees to help you in the restructure process such as identifying issues, coming up with solutions for them and other parts of the process.

Managing the change and handling it effectively

The first step should be to identify the people who are going to be affected by the re-structure process, and train them accordingly so that they know what is going to happen and how it will affect them.

A proper communication plan should be prepared which will give details about the changes, their effects on each individual employee, and what he/she must do during this period while restructuring is being carried out.

This would greatly reduce confusion among employees regarding what exactly is happening, why it has happened and how it will affect them. It would also help them in understanding how they should work under the new structure without any ambiguity or confusion arising out of it.

Even though you have informed them previously about the changes, there still may remain some doubts regarding those changes which may arise during this period of time when they see things changing and not going according to their expectations. This is where a clear chain of command will come in handy, as it will help in reducing confusion and doubts among employees regarding who they should approach for any issues if they arise.

The new structure may also lead to changes in work location of employees, and this could cause problems if not handled properly. To deal with this, you can prepare a plan in advance to give clarity about the work location of each employee after the restructure process is complete and how it will be managed.

You should also remember that people may have different concerns regarding the restructure process such as financial security, performance appraisal, and other crucial things, which are important factors but cannot be managed by you directly, so you should make sure that you have a clear communication plan prepared which gives details about these concerns to the concerned people, so they do not feel cheated or uncertain about their future prospects.

During this whole process, there is always high probability of some people being dissatisfied with the changes being implemented, and they may even oppose them actively or passively through various ways, so it is important to ensure that these people are identified beforehand and dealt with properly as per your communication plan so that they do not create problems in the process of restructuring.

In today's times, every organization has a huge IT infrastructure which is used for various purposes such as storing data, managing files, communication and other services. This can be a big challenge while case re-structuring is being done and other departments are being amalgamated or merged into one larger department, as this could give rise to issues regarding different IT systems which are being used by employees working under different departments. It is important to have a clear plan in place regarding how these systems will be integrated or managed, so no problems arise due to them, and the new system gets implemented smoothly without any hiccups.

You should also have a proper plan in place for making sure that the new structure does not create any problems while work is going on. For instance, if there are some changes related to reporting structure or hierarchy, it would be very important to ensure that these changes do not lead to confusion among employees about who they should report to in case of any issue or problem which arises during their work. This can lead to a lot of confusion among employees which may affect their productivity levels negatively as well as create dissatisfaction among them leading to more issues such as low employee morale.

It is also important to keep track of the progress made in the restructuring process, as it may be a long process, and there are chances that some issues or problems may arise during this process which require quick action from your end to resolve them. This can be done by setting up a progress tracking system which will give you details about how the restructure is progressing and provide you with real time information about how everything is going on. This will also help you in taking quick action if some issues arise during this process, so they do not go out of hand and cause certain problems.

Mitigating the restructuring effects on employees

It is important to make sure that all employees are informed properly about what exactly is happening, why it has happened and how it will affect them during this restructuring process. One should try to make changes easier for them by giving them enough time to adjust to the changes without any burden on their part in terms of extra work or other responsibilities. If that happens, they would be more worried about these new changes rather than focusing on their work which would lead to a negative impact on their performance.

You should also make sure that employees are not worried about their prospects, because if they are not able to adjust to the new structure, and they do not have a good career prospect, then they may leave the organization. This will affect your organization's performance. This can be done by keeping your communication plan very transparent, so employees know what is going on regarding promotions, performance appraisals, pay raises or any other career related issues. This will help them in understanding the new structure better and will also give them an idea about how it will affect them in future in terms of their career prospects.

It is also important to make sure that employees do not feel uncertain about their financial security, as financial security is an important factor which affects people's decision of staying with an organization or leaving it, so people should feel confident about their financial security even after the restructure has been implemented successfully, so they do not feel cheated or uncertain about their prospects. This can be done by giving details about performance appraisal, pay raises or any other benefits which you give to your employees for doing good work such as additional compensation for overtime work, extra bonuses at the end of the year, promotion to a higher position, and other potential rewards.

Another important thing to keep in mind during restructuring is the way you communicate with your employees and stakeholders. Communicate with them in an honest way, so they do not feel threatened by these changes, and even if they feel threatened by these changes, at least they can trust you as their employer and respect your honesty and transparency in handling them honestly while communicating with them.

A lot of new policies may be implemented during this process which may seem unfair to some of the employees who have been working longer than others, but they should be put in place. It will help in maintaining your organization's standards and give the right message to your employee that everyone is treated equally under this new structure, even if some people are better performers than others. That does not mean that they will get better benefits or rewards than others.

Re-organizing

This is usually undertaken to ensure that the business is run in the most effective manner possible. This is often done when an organization has undergone considerable change or expansion. It ensures that everyone knows where they fit into the organization, what their responsibilities are and how they relate to one another.

When faced with a re-organizing situation, it is important to get the information right. There are many ways to do this, and, of course, some will be more efficient than others.

For instance, one way would be to go around and ask everyone you think might have an opinion or some useful information on what is happening in the business and what they think should happen next. This is certainly practical if you have a small group of people that you can easily gather. It may be very slow if there are hundreds of people you need to talk to, or it may be possible but very expensive if you need to talk to people in other parts of the country or world.

Another way would be for the senior leadership team or executives in general to appoint someone (or themselves) over all the HR functions and give those people the responsibility (and authority) for managing change and developing policies based on their understanding of business strategies, goals and needs.

It's important that whoever is put in charge knows what they are doing; otherwise, there will be chaos. They should have sufficient knowledge about managing change and developing human resource policies so that they understand:

- The opportunities available by changing from one system to another.
- The costs involved in changing from one system to another.
- The potential dangers in changing from one system to another.

Differentiation

This refers to changes that have been made within an organization to make it more distinctive and identifiable in relation to its competitors. This can be through creating new products or services or by altering existing ones.

The marketing functions of the business will often undertake differentiation to promote a brand or product as being different from its competitors. In many cases, though, differentiation does not just affect marketing, but it also extends into other areas such as manufacturing, distribution, and sales processes and procedures.

It is therefore important for HR departments within organizations to engage with other departments to ensure that any changes meet the needs of all the stakeholders within the business.

For example, a company's management team may decide to enter a new market, and therefore it will need to alter its products or services to meet the needs of the new target market as well as changing its marketing strategy.

This change could affect employees by changing their working hours or their role within the business. The HR department would then need to liaise with other departments to ensure that any changes are communicated clearly and effectively throughout the business so that all employees are aware of any forthcoming changes.

The HR department may also be involved in determining how any changes will be communicated. They can ensure that communication is fair and transparent, and make sure that any new policies or procedures are consistent throughout the organization.

For an organization's employees to achieve their full potential, it is important for them not only to be clear about what is expected from them but also how their performance will be measured against certain standards.

One of the key responsibilities of an HR manager is therefore ensuring that any standards they set are realistic and achievable as well as making sure that they are communicated clearly, so employees understand what standards they must meet for their performance to be satisfactory.

Managers within an organization are also responsible for developing strategies and plans of action to help their employees achieve the required standards. This may involve setting out training and development programs as well as giving regular feedback to employees to provide them with constructive feedback about their performance.

For an organization to achieve its objectives, it is important for employees within the business to be aware of the goals and objectives of the organization and how they can contribute towards these.

This therefore involves making sure that employees are fully involved in decision making processes within the business, so they understand how their role fits into the overall objective of the organization.

This also includes communicating any changes made within an organization, so all employees are aware of what is expected from them as well as letting them know why any changes have been made and how these will affect them.

Increasing efficiency

This can be done in several ways; it could involve increasing the level of automation within the business. This may have an impact upon the work that is carried out by line managers. It may also involve making changes to the way in which a particular job or function is carried out. In some cases, changes may also be made purely to increase performance.

For example, a company may decide that an area of their business is underperforming, so they will look into the reasons why. This may involve a study of the work carried out in the area, which could lead to changes in the way that this work is carried out, or who carries it out. It may also require changes to the equipment which is used in carrying out this work.

Another way of increasing efficiency within a business can be through reducing costs, for example, by carrying out internal audits on staff and looking at what they are doing and why. The business can then make decisions to cut down on unnecessary expenditure, for example, by getting rid of some staff members if necessary.

Restructuring and Downsizing

One of the most difficult aspects of managing change is the human impact. It's no wonder- people have a tendency to become deeply involved in their work and to feel secure in their jobs. When downsizing occurs, this security is shattered, and employees must not only be informed of the need for restructuring, but they have to be convinced that these changes are beneficial.

Some people will resist change; others will welcome it with open arms.

Change can take many forms: mergers, acquisitions, divestitures, expansions, or contractions. The process can be painful for everyone; from the CEO to the front-line employee.

The key lies in developing a strategy for coping with change. It's true; some people thrive on change, while others do not. Employees must be convinced that downsizing is necessary, and their needs and desires will be met during the transition period. The process should include:

Communication

Before downsizing occurs, communicate to employees about the reasons for it. Explain how it fits into the company's overall strategy and what benefits it will bring to everyone involved including customers and shareholders. For example, if a company must downsize because of declining profits or products, employees should understand that these conditions are not within their control but are due to economic factors outside of their control. If layoffs are necessary, explain why they are occurring and how they will help improve efficiency in other areas of business operations. Explain why some employees must be laid off, while others are retained.

Empowerment

When making difficult decisions regarding who will remain in the organization and who will leave, there is room for emotion or personal bias to enter the decision-making process. To minimize this possibility, give employees as much input as possible concerning who should stay or go. If the company is downsizing, for example, employees should have a voice in the decision-making process.

As much as possible, be open and honest with employees about your reasoning for the changes that are being made. The more input you get, the better decisions you can make.

You don't want to alienate your employees; remember that they are part of your organization, and they have to believe in what you're doing if you want everyone to be successful in the end. This will take time and patience; it's not something that happens overnight. Explain why change is happening, how it will benefit everyone, and what role each employee must play in helping make it a success.

Reward

Once downsizing has been completed and efficiency has been improved, reward employees who have played a positive role during this difficult period. Recognize their efforts with public praise, bonuses or both. Let them know that their hard work is appreciated, and their efforts are vital to the success of the organization. These positive gestures will encourage employees to continue working hard on behalf of the business even if more cuts must be made or changes need to occur down the road. In addition, this gesture reinforces your company's commitment to its employees which can have a positive impact on morale.

Human Resource Planning Principles

Human resource planning is the process of analyzing the firm's current and future human resource requirements and then determining how to meet these requirements. It is a dynamic process that involves considering the organization's strategic objectives, its internal environment, the external environment, and then formulating strategies to achieve these objectives.

While it is not possible to do effective human resources planning without taking into consideration the external environment in which companies operate (e.g., economy, competitors), internal factors also play a significant role in any organization's human resource planning. The internal factors include:

Financial performance

This includes the company's financial performance during the previous year together with plans for future financial performance. This will help determine if additional employees are needed to help achieve business objectives or if some employees may need to be laid off due to financial constraints.

For example, if the company's financial performance during the previous year was very poor, companies will have to make significant changes to improve their financial performance. This may include reducing workforce and reducing wages or bonuses.

In addition, if a company achieved a significant improvement in its financial performance during the previous year, it may decide to increase employees' wages or give them bonuses as a reward for their contribution to the firm's financial success.

Strategic plans

The company's strategic plans are based on its vision and mission. It also includes the goals that the company has set to achieve its vision and mission. This will help determine if additional employees are needed to fulfill these goals, or if some employees may need to be laid off due to the lack of job requirements.

For example, if a company has a vision to become one of the best companies in its industry, it will have several strategic plans (e.g., improve on customer services, improve on product quality and performance). If such strategic plans require additional employees to be achieved, then human resource planning will have to determine how many additional employees are needed, their qualifications and skills required for these jobs as well as how much it would cost.

In addition, human resource planning will have to consider where these new employees should be located (e.g., offices or factories) and what would be the most appropriate compensation package for each employee. The analysis of these factors is crucial not only for achieving strategic objectives but also for keeping the organization financially stable (i.e., avoiding bankruptcy).

Policies and Procedures

A policy is a statement of management's position on an occupational, industrial, or other matter such as pay, benefits, safety, and other crucial things. It is a document usually prepared by top management that sets standards of conduct for employees and provides direction and guidance for their activities.

A procedure is a set of directions or instructions describing how a task should be done. It is a step-by-step method of accomplishing it.

Policy statements are generally drafted by the human resources department while procedures are developed by the operations managers in their departments as part of the company's operations manual.

Policy and Procedure Examples:

- The company has a policy that states employees must work on holidays but only when it is essential that the job gets done. Employees are not to be forced to work on holidays.
- The human resources department has a procedure for the employee benefits program. It describes the various benefit programs, how to enroll, and how benefits can be used.
- The operations department has a procedure describing how to return defective products to the supplier and requests for new products from the production facility manager.

Policy and Procedure Development Tips:

- The human resources department should develop policies and procedures that affect the entire company, such as the employee benefits program policy and procedure example.
- The operating departments should develop policies and procedures that affect only a certain job function within the company. This will ensure that each employee has a copy of the policy and procedure for his or her job function.
- The HR department should establish a system to monitor all policies and procedures to ensure compliance with them.
- Management should encourage employees to use policies and procedures as guides for their activities. If employees do not follow the policy or procedure, then they must be disciplined accordingly.

Pregnancy and Maternity Leave Policies

HR managers or business owners must allow an employee to take pregnancy and maternity leave of up to 15 weeks. The leave is paid at the employee's regular wage rate.

When the employee has multiple births (twins and triplets), the leave is increased by 5 weeks for each additional birth. When an employee takes pregnancy and maternity leave, she may also take an extended leave of absence if she has been employed by her employer for at least 6 consecutive months.

The requirement to pay the employee's regular wage rate does not apply to that portion of a leave taken by an employee as part of an extended leave of absence. An employer may not terminate or lay off a pregnant woman because she asks for pregnancy and maternity leave or because she refuses to work while receiving pregnancy and maternity leave.

Employers are required to keep the medical information they receive about employees confidential during their pregnancies.

Job Security

An employer may not terminate or lay off an employee because she is pregnant or because of her pregnancy-related disability. An employer may not discriminate against an employee for reasons relating to pregnancy or a pregnancy-related disability (including medical leave) or deny an employee the same terms and conditions of employment that are available to others who are not pregnant. An employer must accommodate the needs of an employee for reasons relating to pregnancy, childbirth, recovery from childbirth and any related medical condition in the same way it accommodates other temporary disabilities. This includes providing leave for prenatal care and recovery from childbirth. The amount of leave required for this purpose should be no less than what is required by federal law under the Family and Medical Leave Act (FMLA).

An employer is required to hold open a job for a woman who takes pregnancy and maternity leave until she can return to work following the birth of her child. The employer does not have to create a position for her if there is still a need for that position after she returns from leave.

Lactation Support

It is unlawful for an employer to discriminate against an employee for breastfeeding or expressing breast milk. An employer is required to provide reasonable break time for a woman to express breast milk and a private place other than a bathroom in which to do so. A reasonable break time must be paid and cannot be deducted from the employee's normal lunch period.

It is encouraged that employers provide a private space, other than a bathroom, for an employee to express breast milk. However, if an employer allows employees to take breaks, the employer must allow employees to take breaks to express breast milk. The break time taken by the employee must be paid by the employer and cannot be deducted from the employee's normal lunch period.

If an employee is lactating, she must be allowed ample time and a private place (other than a bathroom) to express milk or pump her breasts so that she can maintain her milk supply. The time needed for this purpose is usually about 15 minutes each workday and should not be counted as working time. The place used for this purpose must be comfortable and safe. A refrigerator can be used if it keeps the milk at the right temperature. An employer cannot make any special rules about how employees use their break times or any other working time for breastfeeding or expressing breast milk unless required by law or to protect workplace safety.

Employers are required to provide reasonable accommodations for employees who are lactating or expressing breast milk in order for them to perform their jobs. If necessary, employers should try to find ways to make sure that women who are nursing have enough breaks and places in which they can express breast milk. In addition, employers should pay employees for the breaks taken for breastfeeding or expressing breast milk.

Employee Training and Development Plans

The employee training and development plan is a tool for managing employee development activities. It is a strategic document that contains the organization's approach to identifying, developing, and retaining the workforce. An employer must establish a training policy that describes how it will fulfill its legal obligations to employees concerning training and development. This policy must be consistent with the employer's goals, objectives, and performance standards:

The needs assessment that identifies the effectiveness of current training and development programs.

A description of the training needs of employees based on their skills, competencies, knowledge, and experience. It is also important to identify any gaps in their training and recommendations for addressing those gaps.

An action plan for meeting training needs in a cost-effective manner. The action plan should be consistent with the employer's mission, goals, values, long-range plans, and budget. It should address:

- how to coordinate internal training efforts with other internal programs
- how to coordinate external training efforts with other external programs
- how to provide guidance for self-directed learning

- how to maintain records on employee progress
- how to recognize employees who complete relevant certification or licensing requirements and/or successfully complete formal education or job-related research
- how to use outside providers and
- how to evaluate existing programs or introduce new ones

The following elements are needed when creating a comprehensive employee training and development plan:

Employer's Mission, Goals and Values Statement

The employer must communicate its mission and values through vision statements, strategic plans, and statements of purpose that demonstrate a clear statement of why the organization exists. The employer must also communicate performance expectations and standards for all employees. This can be done through performance reviews that are based on clear job descriptions or other evaluation tools.

Organizational Analysis

In preparing its employee training plan, an organization should perform an analysis of its strengths, weaknesses, opportunities, and threats (SWOT) to maximize its effectiveness in achieving its goals.

This process also helps identify system weaknesses or gaps that may require additional training to ensure organizational success. The result of this analysis should be communicated to employees in a manner that allows them to capitalize on the opportunities available to them while at the same time minimizing any risks they may face from identified threats.

This can be accomplished by helping employees understand how their individual roles impact organizational success and how their contributions affect their organization's goals.

Needs Assessment

An effective training plan is one that helps the organization accomplish its goals by addressing the needs of its employees. The needs assessment should address:
1. the effectiveness of current training and development programs
2. the employee skills, competencies, knowledge, and experience, and
3. recommendations for addressing any gaps in training.

This assessment should be part of an overall organizational analysis that identifies strengths, weaknesses, opportunities, and threats (SWOT).

Employee Training Program

An effective employee training program is one that provides employees with the skills they need to perform their jobs effectively. This program must be consistent with an organization's mission, goals, values, long-range plans and budget. The most effective training programs are those that are aligned with strategic business objectives.

Action Plan

An action plan should include a description of how to coordinate existing internal training efforts with other internal programs such as performance management systems or other performance improvement initiatives. It should also address how to coordinate external training efforts with other external programs such as vendor products or services or industry specific educational offerings. The action plan must provide guidance for self-directed learning by identifying ways to meet the ongoing needs of employees who can no longer attend formal training classes due to their job responsibilities or because they are no longer employed by the organization.

The action plan must address how to maintain records on employee progress by documenting employees' training experience and by using a recordkeeping system that provides training data in a format that can be used to support the needs assessment process.

It must also address how to recognize employees who complete relevant certification or licensing requirements and/or successfully complete formal education or job-related research. The action plan should also include how to use outside providers, such as educational institutions, industry associations, vendors, or consultants.

Finally, the action plan should include how to evaluate existing programs or introduce new ones based on organizational analyses of strengths, weaknesses, opportunities, and threats (SWOT).

Employee Performance Goals

An employee performance goal may be part of an overall performance management system and should be aligned with the organization's strategic goals. It should also be linked with an employee's performance expectations that are defined by their position description and performance standards.

Employee Training Evaluation

An employer must evaluate its training efforts based on its needs assessments as well as any information it receives from employees about their satisfaction with the current training programs. This evaluation should identify ways to modify existing programs as necessary based on these findings.

Here is an example of a comprehensive employee training and development plan.

Employer's Mission Statement:

"At Acme Corporation, the quality of our product is our most important competitive advantage. To ensure consistent, high quality products, we must ensure that the skills of all our associates are developed to meet the requirements of our customers. Our goal is to achieve a state of continuous improvement in every process we undertake."

Organization's Goals, Objectives, and Culture:

"In order to meet customer needs, Acme Corporation must provide its employees with the skills necessary for them to perform successfully. Our training efforts will be aligned with our strategic goals and objectives as well as the company's vision statement. Training will be provided by internal staff or third-party vendors. The company's culture must support these efforts for training to succeed."

Needs Assessment:

The following chart presents an assessment of current training programs at Acme Corporation. The assessment was conducted based on an analysis of how well these programs aligned with organizational goals and objectives as well as the organization's vision statement (See "Organization's Goals, Objectives and Culture" above). The results of this assessment should be used to identify gaps in employee knowledge, skills and competencies that have the potential to impact organizational success.

In addition, the organization should conduct an analysis of its strengths, weaknesses, opportunities, and threats (SWOT) to maximize its effectiveness in achieving its goals. This process also helps identify system weaknesses or gaps that may require additional training to ensure organizational success.

Training Program:

Acme Corporation will continue to use a combination of instructor-led classroom training, web-based seminars, and self-directed learning as part of its overall training efforts. The company uses a formal performance management system to provide employees with the skills they need to perform their jobs effectively. This program must be consistent with Acme's mission and vision statement as well as the organization's strategic goals and objectives (See "Organization's Goals, Objectives and Culture" above).

Action Plan:

The following action plan is designed to address current training needs based on the results of the needs assessment presented in the chart above ("Needs Assessment" section). In developing this action plan, Acme Corporation used the following guiding principles:

1. The company will use a combination of instructor led classroom training, web-based seminars, and self-directed learning as part of its overall training efforts. The company has chosen this combination because it will maximize the effectiveness of its training efforts.

2. The company will use a formal performance management system to provide employees with the skills they need to perform their jobs effectively. This system is aligned with Acme's mission and vision statement as well as the organization's strategic goals and objectives (See "Organization's Goals, Objectives, and Culture" above).

3. Training will be provided by internal staff or third-party vendors. The company has chosen this combination because it provides a cost-effective alternative to maintaining an in-house training

department when compared with using only internal staff. This allows the company to focus on its core competencies while providing quality training at a reasonable cost.

Sample Training and Development Plan

Acme Corporation Employee Training and Development Plan:

Acme Corporation's employee training program focuses on ensuring that employees have the following skills:

1. Product Knowledge - Acme Corp.'s products are highly technical in nature and require specific knowledge that not all employees possess when they are hired into their jobs. Therefore, employees must be trained in these areas prior to assuming their jobs or as soon as possible after being hired into their jobs. The company relies on its managers to ensure that new hires complete this initial product training within two weeks of being hired.

2. Customer Service - The company's mission and vision statement emphasize the importance of customer service to overall organizational success. Therefore, the organization's training program will ensure that all employees are trained in customer service skills. This training will be incorporated into other training courses as appropriate.

3. Problem Solving - The company believes that its employees must be able to solve problems if they are

to achieve organizational goals and objectives. Therefore, the organization's training program will ensure that all employees are trained in problem solving skills so that they can effectively respond to any issues that arise during the execution of their jobs or other tasks assigned by their managers or other individuals who are responsible for overseeing them on a day-to-day basis (i.e., team leaders or supervisors). This training will be incorporated into other training courses as appropriate.

Employee Performance Goals:

Acme Corporation uses a performance management system as part of its overall performance improvement efforts (See "Action Plan" above). This system provides employees with performance goals for each employee review cycle and links these goals with individual responsibilities identified in each employee's position description and/or job description. As such, these goals should be aligned with individual responsibilities and job descriptions.

Employee Training Evaluation:

The company uses an employee survey to measure the effectiveness of its training efforts. The results from the surveys are used to assess how well the organization is meeting its overall objectives and to identify any weaknesses that may exist in the organization's training efforts. This survey also allows employees to provide feedback on the quality of their training as well as their satisfaction with the current training programs. This information will then be used to modify existing programs or introduce new ones, as appropriate.

Workplace Flexibility Policies

Choosing to implement a flexible workplace policy can improve morale, reduce absenteeism, and increase job satisfaction. Employees increasingly consider flexible work options when deciding where to work. In fact, one recent survey found that nearly 75 percent of employees say they would consider leaving a job if it didn't offer flexible work options.

Today, many organizations are making work-life balance a priority. Employers are offering flexible work schedules, telecommuting options, and other flexible work arrangements as ways to attract and retain employees. In addition, many employers are creating these arrangements for existing employees in an effort to retain valuable talent and address role conflict.

Many factors drive an employer's decision to implement a flexible work arrangement program. The employer may want to tailor its policy to meet the needs of some of its employees, or it may want to create a more inclusive workplace culture. Whatever the reason, implementing this type of program takes careful planning and consideration.

Many companies already offer some form of workplace flexibility. In fact, some companies have offered flex-time or telecommuting programs for several years.

Flexible Work Options

- Flex-time: Allowing employees to adjust their regular work schedule to better accommodate family and personal obligations
- Telecommuting: Permitting employees to work from home
- Alternative work schedules: Rotating shifts, working four 10-hour days each week, or taking periodic paid time off during the workweek (compressed or block schedule)
- Job sharing: An arrangement where two people share a single job but don't necessarily have identical hours.
- Job swapping: Arranging for employees to swap jobs with other employees so they have an opportunity to learn new skills. They may also swap jobs with other departments within the organization.
- On-call scheduling: Asking an employee to be on-call during certain periods, such as evenings and weekends, for possible call-back. This might be a condition of employment for shift workers at a hospital, fire station or police department.

Implementing a Flexible Work Arrangement Program

The first step is to create a detailed plan outlining your goals for the program and how you intend to implement it. This document should include written policies that outline how various types of flexible work arrangements will be offered as well as how they will be managed (i.e., who will manage them, who can take advantage of them, and other such roles). This is where you need to define what you mean by "flexibility". For example, do you intend on allowing time off or paid time off?

Do you allow telecommuting? Do you allow employees to change their schedule?

The second step is to communicate the program to employees. Include a detailed description of the program and how it is expected to be administered in your employee manual. Make sure you include information about which positions will be eligible for flexible work arrangements as well as which positions will not be eligible. Additionally, you should also provide information on how employees can take advantage of these programs. If there are policies against favoritism, make it clear that this type of flexible workforce is meant to allow all employees to benefit from a more inclusive work environment regardless of their status within the organization.

While implementing the flexible work arrangement program, it's important that you educate managers on how they should handle requests for flexibility from their employees. You can accomplish this by providing managers with a document outlining all the details of your flexible work arrangement program. This includes detailed guidelines and best practices for managers when communicating with their employees about these programs. This will help ensure consistency across your workforce and across different organizational departments and levels.

Creating policies outlining how your organization will offer its employees flexible work arrangements is an important first step in implementing a successful flexible workforce program. However, it's also crucial that your organization has a well-defined plan that provides employees and managers with the information they need to manage and maintain a flexible workforce.

Chapter 4: Linking Compensation to Company Strategy

In order to be effective, compensation programs must be linked to the organization's strategy. The program should support the firm's mission and objectives by supporting its primary goals and objectives. Thus, compensation programs should enable the organization to accomplish all its business goals by:

- Enhancing employee loyalty
- Enhancing productivity
- Improving performance in key areas where the firm needs to excel
- Performance-based compensation programs

Compensation programs that are linked to the organization's strategy should be designed to motivate employees to produce and achieve desired results. The most effective program will be one that provides incentives for employees to excel in their jobs.

This can be accomplished through a performance-based compensation program that is designed to reward superior performance and success. It may include a combination of cash, stock options, and/or stock purchase plans, as well as other types of non-cash awards.

By linking compensation directly to the achievement of organizational goals, organizations can increase employee motivation and improve productivity.

A Performance-Based Compensation Program Works by:

- Motivating employees with money and other benefits that are tied directly to the achievement of organizational goals.
- Providing a mechanism for rewarding employees who have performed above expectations or who have contributed significantly to the success of the organization.
- Providing a mechanism for rewarding employees who contribute to the success of a business unit, department, or other work unit.
- Providing an incentive for employees to perform at higher levels and excel in their jobs.

A Performance-Based Compensation Program Does Not Work by:

- Tying compensation to the personal goals of an individual employee.
- Creating expectations that cannot be met by the employee. For example, it is not realistic to expect an employee to consistently achieve sales quotas that are twice as high as the average sales quota or to have a perfect attendance record when the organization does not have a policy of paying attendance bonuses.
- Expecting employees to do something that they are not capable of doing. For example, it is inappropriate to pay an employee a bonus for doing something that he would normally do in his job without additional compensation.
- Providing a means for rewarding employees who do not contribute to the success of the organization.

- Providing a compensation program that will not be accepted by employees. If employees perceive that they will be taken advantage of, they will not accept the program and it will have no motivational value.

Compensation should be linked directly to the achievement of organizational goals and objectives and should be designed to improve employee performance. Performance-based compensation plans can provide an incentive for employees to excel in their jobs and increase productivity.

Such programs are particularly effective if managers are encouraged to use performance-based pay as an incentive, rather than using it as the only factor in determining base salaries or total incentives.

Performance-based pay programs can also be used for rewarding entire teams or departments that have performed above expectations or contributed significantly to the success of a business unit, department, or other work unit.

By tying compensation directly to the achievement of organizational goals and objectives, organizations can increase employee motivation and improve productivity without incurring additional costs.

In this chapter, we will examine the following topics above in greater detail.

Employee Benefits: An Overview of Major Programs

Employee benefits are an important part of your total compensation strategy. Benefits can help you attract and retain quality employees, and they can also provide an important incentive to employees who remain with you.

Benefits have two primary functions

They must be competitive with the compensation programs offered by other companies in your industry. They must be directly tied to the goals of your organization and may include a variety of programs that are designed to attract, retain and motivate employees.

Benefits can be categorized in numerous ways, but (for simplicity's sake) we will divide them into three major categories:

Group Benefits

These are employer-paid programs that are generally administered by a third party (e.g., Blue Cross or United Health Care). Group insurance is probably the most common employee benefit, but there are also other group benefits such as life insurance or disability insurance policies that may be purchased for your employees.

The advantage of group benefits is that they are generally cheaper than individual policies purchased through an agent or broker, since the cost of administration is spread over all participants in the plan. Since individual employers bear much of the cost for administration, some employers choose not to purchase group policies at all and instead offer their employees an employer-paid individual insurance policy.

Individual Benefits

These are benefits that employees directly pay for on their own, and they may or may not be administered by a third party (e.g., dental insurance is an individual benefit, while an HMO is a group benefit).

Employee Assistance Programs (EAPs)

These are benefits that employees pay for on their own, but include assistance from you in obtaining the service (e.g., a money management program provided by you through a bank). EAPs can provide valuable assistance to your employees in resolving personal financial problems.

Here are some of the most common types of employee benefits:

Medical Insurance

This can be an expensive program, but it is one of the most important benefits you can offer your employees. Medical insurance covers many common medical costs such as doctors' visits, hospital stays and prescription drugs. It also typically covers some less common medical expenses such as long-term care and accidents as well as dental expenses.

You will need to choose between two basic types of medical plans:

- preferred provider organizations (PPOs) or
- health maintenance organizations (HMOs)

PPOs allow members to go to any doctor or hospital that participates in the plan, while HMOs require members to use doctors assigned by the insurance carrier.

A third option is a high-deductible health plan (HDHP), which combines a deductible with a lower premium than traditional plans.

Dental Insurance

This is another very important group benefit that covers dental expenses such as cleanings, fillings, and crowns.

Vision Insurance

This can be an inexpensive way to cover the cost of eyeglasses and contact lenses.

Life Insurance

This is designed to cover the financial needs of your employees' families in the event of death or disability.

Disability Insurance

This covers some of the expenses associated with temporary disabilities, such as lost wages from missed work, medical costs, and rehabilitation expenses.

Retirement Savings Plans

These are generally employer-matching contributions to retirement accounts that you make available to your employees through an employer-sponsored retirement plan (e.g., 401k or 403b).

Employee Stock Ownership Plans (ESOPs)

These are plans where the employer will match a portion of employee contributions into company stock which vests over time, so employees feel more vested in their workplace.

Health Clubs/Fitness Centers

These programs provide your employees with access to on-site exercise facilities.

Child Care

These include programs that allow you to keep your children on the company's health insurance while allowing you to go back to work.

Combining base pay and incentives

Compensation in the form of base pay and incentives should be linked closely to the company's overall performance. When this linkage is not present, the compensation system can become ineffective or even destructive because it can send employees the wrong message.

For example, poorly designed incentive systems are a major reason why many companies lose their best employees. Incentive programs that encourage individuals to maximize short-term results at the expense of long-term results often cause employees to act in ways that hurt the overall performance of the company.

For example, a salesperson may concentrate on selling products with high commissions instead of focusing on developing long-term customer relationships. The salesperson's short-term focus may result in higher commissions for that salesperson (and perhaps higher earnings for other salespeople), but it is unlikely to do much for company profitability or long-term market share.

A more serious problem arises when some members of management also focus on generating short-term profits (for themselves rather than for the company) by eliminating unprofitable lines or by laying off productive employees. Such management behavior has caused many companies to operate at less than full capacity during periods when they should be expanding their businesses and adding new products and services.

Managers who are compensated with incentives must be compensated according to the company's performance. When the company does well, managers should receive their share of earnings. However, when the company is performing poorly, they should not be rewarded. Employees also need to understand that managers will not receive all their incentive compensation unless the company meets its goals.

Compensation programs that encourage long-term thinking

Compensation programs should be designed to encourage long-term thinking. In addition to pay and incentives, employees should receive generous benefits. Compensation plans can be structured so that employees are rewarded for good performance over the long term. For example, stock options and other equity-based incentives can be used to encourage employees to think like owners of the business.

Stock options are contracts that give an employee the right (but not the obligation) to buy a certain number of shares of company stock at a specified price (called the exercise price). Stock options which are often granted in conjunction with other types of compensation can be very effective in motivating employees and aligning their interests with those of shareholders.

Stock options provide a way for an employee to earn more money if the company does well. The value of stock options will rise as the share price increases, and they may become more valuable when they are exercised than when they were granted.

The two main types of stock option plans are as follows:

Incentive stock option (ISOs)

ISOs allow employees who hold more than 10% of their compensation in ISOs to deduct up to 50% of any gains from its sale before paying taxes on them. This special tax treatment of ISOs is available only for ISOs, and it is not offered in any other type of equity-based incentive plans.

Nonqualified stock option (NSO)

NSOs allow employees to avoid paying capital gains taxes on 50% of its gains from its sale until after the options expire. However, there is no special tax treatment for the remaining 50% of the gain. The employer must withhold income taxes on both the original grant and the exercise price.

Many companies also provide additional incentives to employees through their retirement plans. The most common retirement plans are as follows:

401(k) plan

A 401(k) plan allows employees to defer a portion of their pay until later, when they will receive it either as a lump sum or as a series of payments over time (called annuities). By deferring income, an employee can reduce his or her current tax liability. Such deferred compensation may be paid in either cash or in shares of company stock that were acquired in an employee stock purchase plan (ESPP).

An ESPP allows employees to acquire shares at a discount from their market value when they are purchased with salary reductions or other specified contributions by an employee.

Employees who participate in 401(k) plans pay no taxes on the contributions until they are withdrawn, and they pay no taxes on the gains from the investment in the plan while the gains are reinvested in the plan.

Deferred compensation plans

These plans allow employees to defer a portion of their salary or other compensation until a specified time in the future. Companies may offer deferred compensation plans to attract and retain employees, but these plans can also be used to motivate employees without increasing their overall compensation. Payment of deferred compensation is usually made upon retirement or termination of employment. Some companies use deferred compensation to increase employee motivation and align employee interests with those of shareholders by providing bonuses at specified times in the future instead of paying them immediately.

Stock ownership programs

These programs provide an incentive for employees to buy stock at a discount from its market price by matching some or all their purchases with employer contributions. Employees who participate in stock ownership programs usually receive a percentage - typically between 10% and 20% - of their equity holdings over time based on the company's performance relative to that of its competitors. Stock ownership programs are often combined with other types of equity-based incentives to further encourage employee participation in company stock.

Some companies also use employee recognition programs including cash awards to recognize outstanding performance.

Incentive plan design

The incentive plan design should be logically linked to the goals and objectives of the organization. The incentive plan design should also be linked to the total reward strategy. It should be a part of the total reward strategy, not stand alone.

Incentive plan administration

The design of an incentive plan is one thing, and its implementation is quite another. The rewards earned from any incentive plan should be based on performance that is measured against clearly stated goals and objectives along with reasonable standards for performance evaluation.

Maintaining an effective program requires care in choosing and defining goals and objectives, relating those goals and objectives to the organization's business strategy, establishing company-wide standards for performance evaluation, and monitoring the results throughout the year to ensure that all employees are adequately rewarded for their contributions to organizational success.

Incentive plan administration involves careful award-determination procedures, regular measurement of individual performance against predetermined levels of performance, accurate calculation of awards based on those measurements, prompt payment of awards in a timely manner, continuing attention to changing conditions within each area affected by incentives (such as shifts in market demand or changes in staffing levels), regular review procedures for modifying or deleting programs where they no longer serve their intended purpose and participation by all levels of management in the review of programs.

Incentive plan administration also involves the use of a record-keeping system. This system may be paper-based, computerized, or a combination of the two. Whatever its form, it must be able to support all aspects of the program: with appropriate files for each employee and program and other specialized files such as those for customers and suppliers, with adequate filing space for tracking progress toward meeting goals and objectives, with access for authorized staff to review recent performance records and with procedures in place to ensure confidentiality within the organization. The system must also produce information that is timely, accurate, well organized, readily available to appropriate management staff, and useful in planning future rewards.

The importance of incentives to the success of an organization cannot be overemphasized. The strategic objective of any business, whether service or manufacturing oriented, is to create a competitive advantage that will enable it to offer a product or service at a price and in such a manner that satisfies the needs of its customers. The organization must do this profitably if it is to survive.

The most effective way for an organization to differentiate itself from its competitors and earn higher profits is through the application of human resources management techniques. The use of incentive programs can help an organization accomplish its strategic goals by motivating employees toward greater performance and commitment while fostering employee commitment to the organization's goals and objectives.

Setting up an incentive plan at your company

Setting up an incentive plan at your company and getting employees to agree to the plan is not always easy. Often, there is a complaint that the plan does not pay enough money. The claim is then made that it is not worth the effort. Unfortunately, this type of thinking can be very costly to the organization in terms of lost productivity. Effective use of an incentive plan can result in a lower turnover rate and greater employee commitment to attaining organizational goals and objectives.

Organizations that have a well-designed incentive plan in place are more cost-effective than organizations that do not. These organizations usually demonstrate competitive advantages over their competition. The advantages can be a lower rate of turnover, greater commitment to attaining organizational goals and objectives, greater customer satisfaction and higher profits.

The most important thing in the design of an incentive plan is to make sure that it is linked to the business strategy of your organization. A business strategy may include one or more of the following: expanding into new markets, product or service development, cost containment, improving market share, increasing market share, or improving quality.

In addition to linking with the business strategy of your organization, the incentive plan should also link with other aspects of your total rewards program. Some other aspects may include quality programs and leadership development programs. Therefore, it is important to communicate the requirements for each program to all employees so they understand how each program relates to their jobs and how they can earn rewards from each program.

To design a good incentive plan, you should consider three factors: desired performance levels, rewards for meeting or exceeding performance levels and how rewards will be distributed within the organization as well as how they will be communicated to employees. A desired performance level is the level of performance your organization would like to achieve in the areas affected by incentives.

For example, incentives can be targeted toward a desired sales level or a cost-reduction target. The rewards for meeting or exceeding the desired performance levels should be clearly stated and easy to understand. Rewards for meeting or exceeding performance levels may include additional pay, time off, quality awards and other nonmonetary rewards such as plaques or trophies.

The third factor is how rewards will be distributed within the organization. This includes an analysis of each position's contribution to the overall success of the organization and how much reward that position should receive from each incentive program. The analysis should consider the importance of each position as well as each employee's contribution to organizational success. It should also consider what type of reward would best motivate that employee and what type of reward would have a greater impact on the organization's success.

Communicating with employees

One of the most important aspects of designing an incentive plan is communicating it properly to employees. If you want your plan to work effectively, you must communicate it clearly and often during its design phase and continue doing so throughout its implementation.

This is particularly important in establishing performance standards and determining the amount of reward that employees will receive. Employees will be more motivated to contribute to the success of the organization if they understand how they can earn rewards from each incentive plan and how those rewards will be calculated.

Communicating with employees also involves training them to use your computer system or paper filing system that is needed for tracking progress toward meeting goals and objectives as well as for computing performance levels and reporting results.

How to motivate employees without an incentive plan

"Money is a good motivator, but the money only comes after the work is done." - Peter Drucker

While money does motivate people, it cannot be used as the primary motivator. Only intrinsic motivators can do that. The reason is that extrinsic motivators cannot sustain performance. They only work in the short term and then burn out quickly. To get sustainable performance, you need to develop a culture of intrinsic motivation where employees are motivated by their own internal drive to perform well. This type of employee engagement can be sustained for a long time and results in higher levels of performance than extrinsic motivators can achieve on their own.

Once you have helped your employees develop an internal desire to do well at work, you can provide incentives that they will find meaningful and motivational but that will be secondary to their intrinsic motivation. These incentives should be rewards for achieving specific goals rather than just compensation for time worked or years of service. By tying goals directly to rewards, employees will have an incentive to perform well because they want those rewards rather than because they feel they "have to" perform well to keep their job or get a raise.

The best form of incentive is a combination of financial and non-financial rewards. Financial incentives have the obvious benefit of providing a direct monetary reward that can be used to purchase the things employees value such as new technology, a new car, or travel. Non-financial rewards are things like recognition and praise from management, getting to work on projects that interest you, or having your ideas put into practice.

Compensation budgeting

In this section, we will review the process of determining the total annual compensation to be paid to each employee. Some companies use a combination of salary, bonus, and benefits to calculate total compensation. Some companies use only one component (e.g., salary) or two components (e.g., salary and bonus).

The following is a list of common elements in an employer's annual compensation budget:

Base pay

This is a fixed amount that the company pays its employees on an ongoing basis for their work on a regular schedule during the year. Typically, it consists of an hourly rate for salaried workers and an annual rate for hourly workers. Base pay is often referred to as "fixed pay." Salaries are usually expressed in terms of a monthly rate multiplied by 12, resulting in an annual rate. Bonuses are typically expressed as a percentage of base pay.

Performance bonuses

These are bonuses that are paid to employees based on their performance in some manner such as sales volume, productivity or some other attribute that is within the employee's control.

Productivity bonuses

These are bonuses that are paid to employees based on their productivity. Productivity is typically measured by an analysis of the output of the employee over a period of time. For example, one appliance manufacturer pays a bonus to its production workers based on the number of units produced during a pay period. The company usually maintains a standard target for production and the worker must produce at or above that level to be eligible for the bonus.

Profit sharing

This is a bonus paid to employees based on the profits that they help generate for the company. Profit sharing plans come in many forms but usually include elements such as:

- annual bonuses paid annually to employees based on their contributions,
- additional stock grants granted at predetermined times during the year, often based on percentage of profit earned, and
- additional long-term incentive awards granted either annually or at predetermined times during the year.

One-time cash awards

These are bonuses paid one time only and may be given for any reason, such as an employee's anniversary with the company or some other milestone achieved by that employee (e.g., winning an outside award). These are typically referred to as "special occasion" awards.

Stock options

These are awards given to employees based on the purchase of stock for a future date at a price fixed when the option is granted. Options usually expire sometime in the future and are exercisable only when they expire. For example, an employee may get one option per year for five years and can exercise it at any time during that five-year period if it is still open. Stock options are usually granted as part of an incentive plan (discussed below) and vest over a specified period. For example, an employee may receive 10,000 stock options with 5,000 vesting on each anniversary date for five years. At the end of year one, 5,000 options will become vested for that employee.

The best way to explain the process of budgeting total compensation is to walk you through a sample budget for an employee of a small company. The example we will use is for a sales manager at a small company with annual sales of $10 million.

The first step in determining total compensation is to analyze the job and determine what skill set, knowledge level, and personality traits are required to perform that job. For example, if the job requires that people skills are important, the person in that position will be given more weight when determining total compensation than someone who is good with numbers but does not have good people skills. It may be helpful to ask people who know the individual well (supervisors, peers, subordinates) whether they would be willing to accept less pay if they received more benefits. For example, would they be willing to accept less money if they could choose their own health plan? Remember: More benefits mean higher total compensation!

Once you have determined what level of skill set and knowledge are required for this position you can estimate the cost of training an employee in that position from scratch. This will help you determine what salary base pay should be paid for this position. You may want to use outside resources such as trade magazines or industry associations for help in estimating the cost of training.

The next step is to determine if this position is a member of the company's "critical path" - that is, the key positions that are needed for the company to succeed. If so, you want to ensure that you do not lose this person, as they will most likely be one of your top performers, and it can be very costly to replace them. It would also be helpful to know if there is a limit on how much money an employee can make because of other employees in the organization who are paid strictly by salary and cannot exceed a specific ceiling on compensation.

The following step is to determine what benefits will be offered to this employee based on their base pay. For example, if an employee works 40 hours per week for 50 weeks per year (2,000 hours), their annual gross pay equals $60,000 ($30 per hour times 2,000 hours). The first step in determining benefits costs is to arrive at their annual cost based on an hourly rate. For example:

Cost of benefits[2] = $11.6 / hour X 2,000 hours = $23,200

If you have determined that your employee will be covered under your company's health plan, this will be the first step in determining the cost of benefits. Obviously, you will

---

[2] Devra Gartenstein (updated February 12th 2019), Available from https://smallbusiness.chron.com/cost-employee-benefits-employer-2694.html

pay more if the employee has a family than if they are single. You will also need to determine whether they will be covered under your company's health plan or whether they will have to purchase this coverage independently (e.g., through a spouse or some other source). If they must purchase their own coverage, you need to determine what the cost of this coverage would be and how much it would reduce their compensation package (i.e., what percentage of their total compensation is that benefit costing you).

The next step is to determine if any of the other benefits your company offers can be assigned directly to this person without burdening another employee. These may include:

Company car

If an employee has a company car, there are several approaches that could be taken: (1) The employee could be given a fully paid car and be responsible for all costs associated with it including gas, maintenance, insurance premiums and repairs; (2) The employer could pay for all costs associated with the car but require them to work some number of hours per month (e.g., 60) towards paying for it; or (3) The employer could pay for a portion of the costs associated with the car and require the employee to pay some of the costs directly (e.g., you pay 50% of the cost and they pay 50%).

Paid time off

If an employee has some paid time off, this may be included in their compensation package. For example, some companies will allow employees to accumulate vacation time until they have earned a certain amount of paid time off, at which point, it is paid out to them upon termination. If your company uses this type of policy, you would simply include the cost of that amount in your calculation. For example, if an employee has accumulated 18 days (we will use days in this example) and it costs $300 per day to provide this benefit, you would add $5,400 (18 days x $300 per day) to their compensation package.

Health insurance

Some companies offer health insurance as a benefit. If so, you can assign this value directly to the employee's compensation package[3] based on the cost per month for each employee in that plan or based on how much they are paying in premiums depending on what policy you have implemented with your health plan provider. To determine the potential cost for this employee, you need to know what level of coverage they will be purchasing. For example, maybe they are covered under an individual premium plan and it is costing them $103.50[4] per month. If the employee is covered under your company's group plan and they are paying $501.25 per month for a family of five, then you would add $1,242 per year for an individual or $6,015 for a family for a period of 12 months.

Dental insurance

This may also be offered as a benefit. If so, it can also be assigned directly to the employee's total compensation package. The cost for this benefit will be based on the monthly cost per employee in that plan or what percentage of premium

---

[3] Priyanka Anand (updated December 27th 2016), Available from https://onlinelibrary.wiley.com/doi/abs/10.1002/hec.3452
[4] Amy Fontinelle (updated March 13th 2021), Available from https://www.investopedia.com/how-much-does-health-insurance-cost-4774184

each employee pays. For example, if the monthly cost for this benefit is $25 and there are five employees in that plan (including the person we are analyzing) and each employee pays 20% of the premium (that would mean each one pays $5), then your total cost for this dental insurance benefit would be $250 ($25 x 5 employees). Thus, if your company pays 80% of the premium (20% by each employee), you would assign $200 to this benefit. Your total compensation cost would be $450 ($400 salary + $50 dental), and your total benefit cost would be $350 ($250 dental + $100 medical).

Bonus Plans Best Practices

Here are the following best practices regarding the implementation of bonus plans:

- Ensure that employees are aware of the plan and how it works.
- Give employees time to understand the bonus plan and make a commitment to participate before the end of the performance period.
- Plan to communicate frequently with employees about the plan, especially during the time they are in a bonus period.
- Watch for any signs of confusion or upset among employees about the plan. If a problem is discovered, fix it promptly and completely.
- Be careful not to promise any bonuses that you cannot deliver (such as exclusivity). Also, include provisions for adjusting bonuses over time in response to changing conditions (such as changes in economic conditions). If you decide to make changes, do so only after thorough consultation with employees.

- Remember that changing a bonus plan is not easy – it can impact relationships with employees and can cause resentment if new plans are not carefully explained.
- Don't forget about the importance of communication. Don't assume that employees know what they need to do to earn a bonus. Explain bonus criteria and the process for achieving a bonus as clearly as possible.
- Make sure that you keep good records to document how bonuses are earned and paid to employees.

Bonuses vs. variable compensation plans

Bonuses are based on performance and how well you achieve the goals that are set forth for you. Bonuses are usually company-specific and not industry-specific, because each company is different.

Variable compensation plans can be either short or long term.

Long term plans provide for long term financial growth and security for the employee and his/her family. These plans can be designed to help employees purchase a home, save money for retirement, save money on taxes, and save money on other crucial money factors.

Short term plans are usually designed to help with specific goals such as buying a new car or going on vacation. They can also be designed to provide certain benefits when employees have children or other life changes occur. Some companies use both long- and short-term plans in their programs and/or combine them with bonuses to create more incentive.

There is a never-ending debate regarding the merits of pay for performance.

Both sides have good arguments: the pro side argues that an employee who performs well should be rewarded, and the other argues that employees are already being rewarded as employees; therefore, they should not have to be rewarded again for their performance.

In my opinion, both sides are right. The company is the one who hires you and pays you a salary. The company has a right to determine what you do and whether or not it meets their standards. As an employee, you have a right to feel that your work is appreciated and be rewarded accordingly.

Bonus payment frequency

If an employer makes regular, predictable payments at set intervals (such as weekly or monthly), most employees will find it easier to budget and plan expenses. Consequently, employees may be more likely to remain with the company for a longer period of time.

If an employer pays irregularly, employees will be in a constant state of flux concerning their financial situation. This may make it harder for the employees to plan and budget for expenses and may result in the employees being more likely to seek employment elsewhere.

Payment frequency can also be viewed from the perspective of how readily the employer's payment schedule is known. If an employer's payment schedule is new or unpredictable, some employees may find it difficult to plan and budget expenses.

- Remember that changing a bonus plan is not easy – it can impact relationships with employees and can cause resentment if new plans are not carefully explained.
- Don't forget about the importance of communication. Don't assume that employees know what they need to do to earn a bonus. Explain bonus criteria and the process for achieving a bonus as clearly as possible.
- Make sure that you keep good records to document how bonuses are earned and paid to employees.

Bonuses vs. variable compensation plans

Bonuses are based on performance and how well you achieve the goals that are set forth for you. Bonuses are usually company-specific and not industry-specific, because each company is different.

Variable compensation plans can be either short or long term.

Long term plans provide for long term financial growth and security for the employee and his/her family. These plans can be designed to help employees purchase a home, save money for retirement, save money on taxes, and save money on other crucial money factors.

Short term plans are usually designed to help with specific goals such as buying a new car or going on vacation. They can also be designed to provide certain benefits when employees have children or other life changes occur. Some companies use both long- and short-term plans in their programs and/or combine them with bonuses to create more incentive.

There is a never-ending debate regarding the merits of pay for performance.

Both sides have good arguments: the pro side argues that an employee who performs well should be rewarded, and the other argues that employees are already being rewarded as employees; therefore, they should not have to be rewarded again for their performance.

In my opinion, both sides are right. The company is the one who hires you and pays you a salary. The company has a right to determine what you do and whether or not it meets their standards. As an employee, you have a right to feel that your work is appreciated and be rewarded accordingly.

Bonus payment frequency

If an employer makes regular, predictable payments at set intervals (such as weekly or monthly), most employees will find it easier to budget and plan expenses. Consequently, employees may be more likely to remain with the company for a longer period of time.

If an employer pays irregularly, employees will be in a constant state of flux concerning their financial situation. This may make it harder for the employees to plan and budget for expenses and may result in the employees being more likely to seek employment elsewhere.

Payment frequency can also be viewed from the perspective of how readily the employer's payment schedule is known. If an employer's payment schedule is new or unpredictable, some employees may find it difficult to plan and budget expenses.

This type of bonus is paid at regular intervals, but not necessarily at the same interval as other salary payments. For example, a company might pay bonuses quarterly but pay salaries on a monthly basis. The bonus may be paid on regularly scheduled dates each year or might be linked to performance or other company objectives. In general, paying the bonus on a regular basis provides employees with greater predictability than if it were paid irregularly.

Bonus payments[5] that are not made on a regular basis may be difficult for employees to plan and budget for. If the bonus is only paid quarterly, an employee might not know if they will receive their bonus until the end of every quarter. This makes it hard for employees to know if they will have enough money at the end of a particular month or quarter to meet anticipated expenses.

In addition, if bonuses are paid irregularly, employees may be less likely to remain with an employer because their compensation is unpredictable. For example, if an employee receives a bonus award for $3,000 in one year and $6,000 in another year, the employee could have difficulty planning expenses because they do not know how much they can rely on receiving each year. This may make it more difficult for them to plan ahead and budget the expenses.

In contrast, if an employer pays bonuses on a regular basis, employees may be better able to plan and budget for expenses. The bonus may be paid out on the same day each month, quarter, or year. This will allow employees to better

---

[5] Vinod Gulvady, FAQs on Payment on Bonus Act, available from https://blog.greythr.com/payment-of-bonus-act-applicability-calculation-eligibility .

anticipate when they will receive a bonus award and will provide them with greater consistency in their financial situation. As a result, employees may be less likely to leave their job because of the variability in salary.

This type of bonus is paid at irregular intervals. As a result, employees may have difficulty planning and budgeting expenses because of the lack of predictability associated with receiving this type of compensation. This is especially true if there are no provisions in place that would protect an employee's salary should they not receive the bonus award. However, because these types of bonuses are not predictable or guaranteed earnings, they may be more attractive to some employees who are most concerned about earning more money rather than having more stable income.

Bonuses that are paid irregularly can also cause problems for an employer if it means that all workers must frequently be re-classified as hourly or salaried workers for tax purposes. For example:

Employee A is employed as a salaried worker with a salary of $50,000 per year. This means that the employer will only withhold Federal income tax[6] from Employee A's salary.

Employee B is also employed as a salaried worker with a salary of $50,000 per year. However, Employee B receives an additional bonus every month for $1,000. Because Employee B receives the bonus on a monthly basis, the employer must withhold Federal income tax from the bonus

---

[6] Jean Murray (updated March 16th 2021), Available from https://www.thebalancesmb.com/giving-employee-bonuses-know-the-tax-implications-397631

instead of from the regular salary payment. As a result, Employee B will still receive $50,000 in pay each year but will not receive the entire tally of $12,000 in bonuses due to withholds as Federal Income Tax (20% x 50,000 = $40,000 after taxes). Regarding bonuses for Employee B, a rate of 25% would withhold a total of $3000. Thus, Employee B would receive an additional $9,000 in total rather than $10,000 at the original rate of withholding.

Chapter 5: Internal Communications

Internal communication is a very important factor in an organization's success. It can help streamline the daily operations of an organization and make employees feel that they are part of a team. Internal communication can also prevent employees from leaving the company, and it can increase employee retention.

Internal communications should not be used to promote or sell products to staff members but rather to provide information that will make them better informed about what is happening in the organization. Good internal communication will also prompt staff members to see if they can anticipate any problems or issues within their area of work and then take action on behalf of their company.

Internal communications can be built around two main themes of communication: information and participation. Information is the theme of internal communication that is most likely to be used daily. Many companies have information newsletters. These are often sent out via email, and staff members are encouraged to contribute suggestions or comments about the articles that are included in the newsletter. Participation is when employees are invited to participate in company activities. This can involve staff members taking part in customer service training or taking part in planning meetings with senior executives.

The methods of internal communications include:

- Printed materials such as newsletters, posters, and notices, which provide information vital to a company's continued success;
- Electronic media such as e-mail and websites;
- Seminars and workshops; and
- Employee suggestion schemes.

Internal communications will vary greatly depending on type of organization, but there are some basic principles of internal communication that can be applied to most businesses.

Internal communications should be:

<u>Clear</u>

All internal communications should include a clear statement of information to be conveyed. Employees should understand what they are being asked to do and the benefits that can come from doing it.

<u>Concise</u>

Internal communications should not include unnecessary information, as this can waste employees' time and prevent them from getting the information they need. Information that is redundant or irrelevant should always be avoided.

<u>Convenient</u>

The method of communication used for internal communications must be convenient for staff members; otherwise, they will not use it. Many companies have an intranet site where staff members can find out about company news without having to search different departments or request information from colleagues.

E-mails are also useful for internal communications since they can reach a large number of staff members in just one email address. Companies can also use a variety of social media tools such as blogs, microblogs, Facebook pages, Twitter feeds, and instant messaging to get their messages across quickly and easily to staff members who are on the move or who have busy schedules.

Consistent
Internal communications should be consistent; otherwise, staff members will be confused about the company's policies and procedures. Regular internal communications are a good way to remind staff members of the company's policies and procedures as well as to let employees know about any changes that have been made.

Frequent
The frequency of internal communications should be determined by the type of business and how it is run. However, it is always a good idea for companies to keep staff members updated on what is happening in the company through newsletters, e-mails, or social media sites like Twitter and Facebook. These tools of communication can also be used to ask questions about work tasks, which can help employees get more out of their jobs.

Personal
Internal communications should always include information about individual employees since this can make them feel that they are part of a team rather than just an employee who works for a company. This will also encourage

employees to take responsibility for their own actions since they will feel that they are working together with their colleagues to help the business succeed.

Positive

All internal communications should focus on positive aspects rather than negative ones, since this will make staff members feel better about their jobs. If there are problems or issues within the company, then internal communications should focus on ways in which they can be resolved.

Private

The information contained in internal communications should always be confidential and not shared with outside parties. Staff members are likely to feel more comfortable with sharing information which will help them to do a better job if they know that their privacy will be respected.

Proactive

All internal communications should be proactive rather than reactive. Internal communications can prompt staff members to think about ways in which problems can be resolved before they happen rather than after they have happened.

Engaging Employees

Engaging employees is the process of getting employees to be active in the organization and commit to their work. Employee engagement is closely related to employee motivation. It describes one's emotional investment in a job or organization.

Employee engagement is an indicator of employee satisfaction and dissatisfaction with the work environment. This will have a direct correlation on productivity, turnover and overall profitability of the company.

Factors that correlate with high levels of employee engagement

Ability to contribute
Employees feel as if they can use their strengths every day at work, and that their manager knows them well enough to help them do so. The ability to learn new things at work also contributes to this feeling.

Recognition for doing good work
Employees don't want just a paycheck; they want credit for what they accomplish, whether it's creating a new product, developing a key service or bringing in new business.

The belief that what they do matters
Employees want to know they are contributing to something bigger than themselves.

Freedom to take initiative
Employees want to be trusted to do what they think is right. They don't want to be forced to follow the rules exactly.

Supportive relationships
Employees feel as though their manager supports them, provides feedback and helps them improve. This

contributes to the sense that they can contribute and make a difference.

Self-confidence
Employees feel that they are constantly growing and developing at work, which gives them confidence in their own abilities.

If an organization can effectively engage employees, then they will be more motivated, engaged and productive. These will directly contribute to increased profitability for the organization.

An organization with high levels of employee engagement is a highly motivated workforce that is fully committed towards success. These are valuable assets for any company seeking high levels of growth and profitability.

Achieving High Levels of Employee Engagement

The following are best practices that best illustrate how an organization can achieve high levels of employee engagement:

- Clearly communicate the organization's business and goals.
- Make employees feel their work matters and that they are contributing to something bigger than themselves.
- Set clear expectations for performance, communicate them and reward employees for meeting these expectations.
- Create a culture of feedback where employees are encouraged to provide honest feedback on how the

organization can be improved. The best organizations have an open culture that encourages continuous employee feedback.
- Show employees they are trusted by letting them take initiative within their job roles, encouraging them to experiment with new ideas, and responding favorably when they come up with a good idea. Encourage them to try new ways of doing things. This is one of the most effective ways to get people engaged.
- Develop a culture of opportunity, where employees feel they are growing and developing both professionally and personally. They should see that they are always learning new skills and improving on existing ones. These are the types of organizations that promote high levels of employee engagement.
- Create a work environment where employees feel that their manager supports them, provides feedback, and helps them improve by giving them suggestions, coaching and mentoring as needed. This is the type of organization where employees are engaged and want to work harder to succeed.
- Encourage open communication by creating an organizational culture where employees can openly share their ideas on how to improve the organization, new ways to do things, need for training or other issues that may be important. This is vital in organizations that want high levels of employee engagement.
- Provide recognition for employees who go above and beyond in performing their jobs, whether it's one-time recognition or a performance bonus for exceptional performance focusing on key objectives. This will help motivate their continued commitment towards success for the organization because they will feel as though they are appreciated for their efforts.

Resolving Employee Issues

As an effective HR professional, you may find yourself dealing with employees who have a wide range of concerns. Some of these issues are long-standing, while others arise in the context of a specific situation or incident. An effective HR professional can respond to employee concerns in a way that contributes to the well-being of the organization and its employees.

The purpose of this chapter is to demonstrate how Internal Communications can be used effectively when dealing with employee issues.

Three Key Areas to Address

- What: Employees need information that is relevant and timely. They also need information that provides them with accurate and appropriate responses to their concerns.
- When: The timing must be right for the communication, otherwise it will not be effective.
- How: The methods selected for communicating with employees must be appropriate and consistent with the issue being addressed, as well as accepted by employees who will receive the message(s).

Internal communications are often the first step in managing employee issues. While there are other approaches, the goal of this chapter is to provide an overview of Internal Communications and demonstrate how they can be used to effectively address employee issues.

Common Issues Addressed by Internal Communications

Some of the key issues that can be addressed with Internal Communications include:

- Employee issues that may be affecting the work performance of an employee or employees.
- Conflict between employees, such as disagreements and arguments.
- Issues related to safety and security, such as accidents and workplace violence.
- Workplace attitudes, such as morale or employee retention.
- Workplace change, such as new technology, reorganization, and job elimination.
- Organizational policies, procedures, and benefits.
- Organizational culture.
- Product quality issues.
- Customer complaints.

The specific issue being addressed may determine the approach used to communicate with employees who will be receiving the message(s). For example:

If an HR professional is concerned about a potential safety issue in a particular department within the organization where a number of employees are involved in the same activity (such as manufacturing), it would be appropriate to send out a general bulletin to all applicable employees (e.g., email) regarding this concern so that they are aware of the situation and what they can do to help resolve it (e.g., provide input on how to correct this situation).

If an HR professional is addressing an issue that involves only a few employees (or even one employee), it may be more appropriate to meet with these individuals individually to address their concerns and respond to them more effectively.

When addressing issues with employees, it is important to remember that it is not always possible (or even appropriate) to resolve all the issues being raised. The goal should be to provide the appropriate information so that employees are aware of the situation and what they can do if they have any questions or concerns.

Internal Communications is a key element of the overall HR process, as well as being an important tool for handling employee issues. It may be necessary to use Internal Communications in conjunction with other tools and techniques to address certain issues effectively within your organization.

Tools to Resolve Employee Issues

These are some of the tools that may be used to resolve employee issues when they arise:

- Exit Interviews
- Employee Surveys
- Focus Groups
- Management by Walking Around (MBWA)
- Performance Reviews
- Suggestion Systems
- Town Hall Meetings
- Training and Development Programs
- Union-Management Relations

The Communication Process

An effective internal communication process is essential for an organization to achieve its strategic goals and objectives. It ensures that the right information is provided at the right time in the right place.

However, internal communication is not only about sharing information and ideas. It is about managing employee knowledge and developing partnerships with employees. It is about being transparent, honest, and open, and it also means recognizing and rewarding employees for their contributions.

The effective internal communication process will:

- Increase organizational effectiveness by providing employees with the right information at the right time in the right place.
- Increase employee satisfaction and retention by establishing a two-way communication network between management and employees.
- Improve employee productivity. Employee knowledge is the key to organizational success, and it is important for employees to understand how their work fits into the big picture.
- Help your organization deal with employee issues in a timely manner.

The communication process is the process by which employees receive information and ideas from you.

Here is the best way to understand the communication process:

Information → Message → Communication → Response

The communication process is one way. It starts with information that is processed and becomes a message that is communicated to employees, who then respond with the desired response.

Information is the raw data and facts that you need to communicate to employees. Information can be verbal or written in any form such as memos, e-mails, letters, reports, books, and magazines. Information must be relevant and timely to be useful. If it is not relevant or timely, it will not have any value for your organization. Most companies have policies regarding how information should be handled within the company.

These policies should be clearly communicated to all employees so everyone knows what type of information should be created and how it should be distributed throughout the company. If these policies are not clear, an individual may decide on his or her own how information should be distributed without realizing the negative impact this may have on your organization's ability to achieve its strategic goals and objectives.

Communication refers to the way you plan for and deliver messages about your organization's vision, mission statements, strategies, objectives, and goals to employees in a manner they can understand and relate to their jobs. Communication is the process of sharing information. Communication is the mechanism through which employees receive and process information.

Response is the reaction of the receiver in accordance with received message. A response should be immediate, deferred, favorable or unfavorable. Verbal responses may include asking questions, requesting information, or altering the narrative of a conversation. In general, the nature of response varies on an individual basis.

Four basic aspects to a communication plan

Identify your audience and develop a strategy for reaching them.

This means identifying your target audience, determining how you are going to reach them, determining how you want them to respond to the message, and deciding whether or not you need to develop a series of messages with different messages for different audiences.

Create and deliver messages that are clear and concise.

Your goal is to ensure that your audience understands the message by using words that they will understand, using visuals and graphics that convey your message, and using any other means necessary such as repeating the message until it has been fully absorbed by your audience.

Develop multiple communication plans.

Determine if you need to have more than one communication plan based on your target audience's understanding of the information being communicated and their ability to respond accordingly.

This will ensure that everyone in your organization understands all issues related to organizational operations including employee benefits, job security, and career development opportunities.

The more people who understand these issues the better prepared they will be when dealing with issues such as downsizing or restructuring in which jobs may be eliminated or changed.

Evaluate the effectiveness of your communication process.

This means determining whether your message has been perceived by your audience and whether the intended purpose has been fulfilled. An effective communication process is extremely beneficial for any firm.

Messages and Responses

Message refers to the various means by which information is presented to employees through various forms such as memos, letters, reports, newsletters, and magazines. As stated above, it is important that you make sure that information is relevant and timely, so it has a purpose and value.

When an employee receives an e-mail or memo with no explanation as to why he or she was selected for this information or what the information means to his or her job, this will cause confusion and could lead to negative feelings about management's intentions. You must ensure that your message is clear and concise for it to be effective.

Response refers to how employees respond when receiving a message from management regarding organizational operations (strategy) or changes within the organization (operations).

The response can consist of any number of actions including:

- Changing the way they work.
- Taking no action at all because they do not understand the message or feel that they have no control over changes that are taking place within their department or the organization as a whole.
- Leaving your organization and going to another organization where they feel that their concerns will be addressed and resolved in a timely manner.

Internal communication is an ongoing process in which employees receive and respond to information, which then leads to a change in their behavior (or lack of change) regarding organizational operations and strategic goals and objectives.

This process continues throughout an organization as employees react to changes within their department or operations as a whole, leading to changes in organizational structure, operations, strategies, and objectives.

To ensure that your employees understand this process it will be imperative to use effective communication methods such as:

- Clear and concise memos, letters, reports, newsletters, and magazines that clearly explain to employees how information is relevant to their job.

- Two-way communication via meetings, committees, and surveys, in which all employees can ask questions about issues that are important to them and their department or the entire organization.
- Training seminars and workshops in which employees learn how their jobs fit into the big picture of organizational operations and strategic goals and objectives, sharing ideas about how they can improve their job performance, and other such goals and objectives.
- A communication process in which you respond to employee concerns in a timely manner to ensure that these concerns are addressed and resolved in a manner that is acceptable to both management and employees.
- Providing employees with the necessary information to make informed decisions about their career development, promotions, training opportunities and other beneficial programs through meetings, questionnaires,3..
and other ways of communicating.

Employee knowledge is essential for an organization to achieve its strategic goals and objectives. Employee knowledge will enable your organization to deal with issues such as downsizing or restructuring in a timely manner by ensuring that all affected employees understand what is going on and how they can make the necessary changes within their department or the organization.

In other words, being proactive rather than reactive. It will also provide employees with a sense of ownership over organizational operations instead of feeling like they are on the outside looking in at what is going on within the organization.

Developing a Communications Strategy

The best way to start your communications strategy is to have a conversation with those you work with, internally and externally. This will allow you to better understand what employees and other key stakeholders want to receive from you. It will also help you identify how often they would expect to receive information from you.

Additionally, there are numerous factors that can influence the type of communication that is most effective for your organization, including:

- Social media usage, which is more prevalent among younger generations;
- The size of your organization; and,
- Your company's culture.

Your communications plan should take these into account while deciding on the best way to communicate with your employees and others who are part of your organization's employee family. It will help ensure that your messages get delivered effectively and in a timely manner.

Furthermore, there are several strategies you can use to achieve this objective: quarterly updates, monthly updates, meet and greets, town hall meetings, and communicating with employees on social media. You should decide which one works best for your organization based on your company's size, culture, and location.

The following are five communication strategies that can help you effectively communicate with employees in your organization:

Quarterly Update

Offering a quarterly update to employees is a great way to keep them informed on the status of your operations. This type of communication can be sent via email, but should not be used to communicate urgent or time-sensitive information. It is also important to keep it short and to the point, as employees will likely not have the time to read a lengthy email. You can also include any relevant information in an attachment if you want employees to save and refer to it later. This strategy is particularly useful for large organizations where there are multiple locations or departments.

Monthly Update

Similar to a quarterly update, this type of communication is typically sent via email and ensures that employees receive relevant information on a monthly basis. However, monthly updates may cover more topics than quarterly updates, as they are generally shorter in length and have less content than quarterly updates. You should still keep these short and simple, so they will not take up too much time for recipients to read or for you to write them each month. A monthly update may include topics such as: company achievements, future plans, upcoming events and any relevant information that you feel may be of interest to employees.

Meet and Greet

A meet and greet is a great way to introduce yourself to new employees in your organization. It gives current employees an opportunity to interact with you and helps you get to know them better as well. This strategy is particularly useful for large organizations where there are multiple departments and locations, but it can also be used by smaller organizations who want to improve communication between management and staff members. This type of communication can take place in person or through another medium, such as video conferencing or a webinar. You should discuss what works best for your organization when deciding how to communicate with employees using this strategy.

Town Hall Meetings

Town hall meetings are particularly useful for communicating business updates, employee concerns, and other important news that you want your entire employee population to hear about at the same time. These meetings can help keep employees more informed about what is happening in the organization, as well as help them feel more involved in the decision-making process and connected with each other. The goal of this strategy is to keep everyone in the loop so that they can make better decisions on a daily basis because they have a better understanding of what is happening within the organization. Town hall meetings can be conducted in person or through another medium, such as video conferencing or a webinar.

Communicating with Employees on Social Media

Social media usage has increased significantly over the past few years, and this trend does not appear to be slowing down anytime soon. Many organizations now have official social media accounts where employees can follow updates and get regular updates on what is happening within the organization. Keeping your employees in the loop is so important, as it fosters a sense of community and a feeling that they are part of something bigger than themselves.

As the number of social media platforms continues to grow, you should consider which ones are most appropriate for your organization as well as those that may be used by your employees. This will help ensure that everyone has access to the same information and that the information being communicated is relevant for each individual or group you are communicating with. An alternative approach to using social media is to create an online discussion forum where employees can raise questions or concerns, share ideas, and post comments on various topics.

Remember, the main purpose of communication in an employee management strategy is to keep all members of your organization informed about what is happening within their department or location as well as within their company in general.

Chapter 6: Mitigating Legal Risks in HR

When it comes to a business, Human Resources is a very important department. It's the one place where all the information about a company can be found. All the employee records, personal information, and data they use in hiring workers are kept here. With all this information at their disposal, HR personnel must take great care to ensure nothing wrong gets out of hand.

In this part of the book, we will look at how you can avoid any legal entanglements with the employees of your company. We will also look at some of the major legal issues that are faced by HR managers and how they can handle them.

Since HR is one of the most important departments in an organization, they must deal with several legal issues that arise from time to time. Some legal issues are unique to human resource management and some others arise with the employees of the organization. Let's look at some common legal issues faced by human resource managers and learn how they can handle them.

Information sharing

Companies need to share information with employees, and you can't always put all the information in writing. Sometimes, it is better to have an informal chat or even a video conference. In such cases, it is essential to remember that you are not just dealing with an employee here. You are also dealing with a human being who has the right to privacy.

Employees often feel uncomfortable when they are being videotaped or recorded for internal use only. It is important that you consider this while recording the video conference so that employees don't feel upset about it. You can ensure that the conversations do not go out of control by making sure you have consent from the employees before recording them on camera. This also gives them the freedom to end the video call if they want to at any point of time without making them feel like they are doing something wrong.

It is also essential to know what kind of information should be shared in a meeting or at a video call. It is important to make sure that there is no sensitive information shared during such sessions because if that information leaks out, this will directly damage your company's reputation and hamper your business prospects in the future as well. If you think that a meeting is not the right platform to share certain information, then it might be better to avoid such meetings altogether.

However, avoid this as much as possible because employees have rights to know about important things that are going on in the company. If you are unable to communicate through a video call or a meeting, then it would be better to postpone the entire process for a suitable time in the near future. In actuality, you have to treat your employees well and not just as mere sources of information.

For example, if you are holding a meeting with the employees and you think that some of them might not be interested in the subject, it is better to hold a separate meeting with those employees to give them the information they need. This way, you will save time and get everyone up to speed at the same time.

Though there is a lot of information security out there about what can endanger your business, there are some things that are overlooked. For example, information security is very important for human resource managers as well. They have access to important information about the company's plans, and all of these should be kept confidential as much as possible.

However, it is not enough to just make sure they have access to confidential data. It is also necessary to know how they use this data so that it doesn't end up being leaked out somewhere else. This requires tracking of all employee computer usage by HR managers and supervisors across the organization. It may seem like an invasion of privacy at first, but this way you will ensure that no employee can leak out any sensitive information out there in public scenarios or social networking sites such as Facebook or Twitter.

If you don't want your reputation destroyed by employee leaks or if you don't want to face a major lawsuit, then you have to take these steps. By doing so, you will also be able to make sure that your employees are protected from identity theft as well because most of the identity theft cases originate from information leaks by employees.

Besides the employee leaks, there is another kind of security risk that HR managers must deal with, and it is called *counterfeit HR documents*. It happens when someone copies all your vital HR documents such as employee records and other sensitive information and sells them out for money.

Since this is a legal issue, it is better if you consult a lawyer before taking any steps to protect yourself from this kind of attack because it requires legal knowledge to detect counterfeit documents. However, there are some things HR managers can do on their own such as keeping track of the authorized personnel who have access to important records. In addition, they can also add some symbols or logos at the bottom of their important documents so that their authenticity can be confirmed easily.

How you manage all these legal issues in your business depends on what kind of business you are running and how much money you are making out of it. If your company is doing well and the profit margin is high, then it is not a problem. But if you are running a small business and your only concern is how to pay the salary of your employees each month, then you must take the right measures to avoid any legal issues that may arise.

Privacy, security, and confidentiality

Privacy, security, and confidentiality are some of the most important legal issues with which HR managers have to deal with. With the job of gathering sensitive information about an employee, it is very important that privacy, security, and confidentiality are maintained.

Privacy concerns the rights of an individual to keep his personal information confidential and private. It is a fundamental right of every person. An employer must protect this fundamental right of employees by following all the guidelines laid down by law in handling such private information.

Security refers to how company data is held and dealt with in terms of its protection from any unauthorized access or theft.

Confidentiality refers to how a company keeps its data secret from other companies or individuals who may use the data against it. Confidential data is considered as sensitive information and adequate measures must be taken to protect those prying eyes. These include critical information such as research data and trade secrets.

Data privacy:

HR professionals collect an enormous amount of data about their employees, prospective employees, and customers every day. This data may range from personal information like their age, address, marital status, and other personal information, to work related details like their performance reports, attendance records and other job-related data. All this data needs to be collected legally and stored securely and privately so that it does not fall into wrong hands. Your organization should have a designated person for data privacy and security of such information.

Employee data

Your employees are one of your most valuable assets, and you want to ensure that they are given the opportunity to give their best in their work. To do this, you need to take care of a few things in the best interest of your employees. A legal issue that is faced by all HR personnel is employee data that needs to be protected from outside access. Personal information about an employee such as contact details, salary ranges, performance reports and other internal information, should be handled with care and responsibility. All this information should be stored securely and legally, and any unauthorized access or theft should be avoided at all costs.

HR professionals must ensure that any kind of confidential employee data they handle is strictly protected from unauthorized access or theft. They should also ensure that no third party has access to it without the written consent of the employee concerned. It is also important that this data is not shared with any other person within or outside the organization without proper authorization by the employee concerned or his/her legal guardian in case he/she is not able to give consent.

Human Resources personnel should also ensure that they do not use the information they have about an employee for their personal gain or any other person's gain. They should also be careful to avoid sharing such confidential information with their family members, friends, and anyone else who may misuse it.

Employee performance

An employee may be one of your best assets, but if his or her performance is not up to the mark, then he or she will not be able to give his best in the job. That is why it is important that HR personnel keep a close tab on how well the employees are doing in their job, and how they can help them to improve their performance by providing them with training or any other kind of professional help. It is also important that HR personnel take all necessary steps to motivate employees, so they can give their best in whatever task they are assigned.

Salary packages

Salary packages are another area where legal issues arise for HR personnel as well as employees at times. You must keep in mind that you cannot pay your employees a salary which does not match with industry standards or which is less than what they deserve as per their job profile and responsibilities. On the other hand, you must make sure that you don't pay your employees more than what is required to keep them motivated.

If you are paying an employee more than what he/she deserves as per the industry norms, then you might end up spending unnecessary money on him/her for a job that is not worth it. On the other hand, if you pay less than what the employee deserves, then he/she may not be motivated to give his best in his job and may end up doing an inadequate job which will lead to losses for your company. So, all in all, it is important that you make sure that your salary packages are legal and fair. If you are not sure whether you are doing the right thing or not, then consult an expert legal counsel for help.

Employment contracts and agreements

It is very important to have a good employment contract in place to protect the interests of both the employer and the employee. It is also very important for the each of them to read it carefully and sign it only after they are satisfied with it.

For an employer, the employment contract should clearly define the terms of employment which include salary, leave policies, benefits, compensation for overtime work and other company-related things.

The contract should also clearly state what kind of behavior from an employee will lead to termination. For example, if a company's policy is that any form of theft by an employee will lead to immediate termination, make sure that there is clarity in these clauses.

For employees, too, it is equally important to have an employment contract in place. The contract lets them know all about their rights as employees. It should clearly state how many days' leave they can take every year, how they can get promoted or move up in their career ladder, what kind of bonuses they can expect for performing well at work and other incentives and bonuses.

Proper documentation

It has been observed that employers tend to neglect proper documentation at times, which leads to a lot of legal problems later on. It is important for HR personnel to be very careful about the documentation process and ensure they do not leave any loopholes.

Let us say an employee has completed six months in your organization and you have decided to give them a salary hike. In such a case, you must make sure that you have all the necessary documents in place to prove it. You should be able to show that the employee had completed six months at your organization, and you had given them another increment. If the documentation is very well managed, it will be very easy for you to prove your case if any legal issues arise later on.

Unemployment issues

When an employee loses his/ her job, they will surely be looking for compensation from their employer. It is very important for HR personnel to be aware of all the unemployment laws in their state, so they can make sure that they are not violating any regulations.

Most states will not allow companies to fire employees just because business is bad and make sure that employees are given adequate compensation when they lose their jobs due to factors such as business issues. This compensation might include severance packages, insurance cover, unemployment benefits or other things involved with termination. Be sure to check with your state labor department and comply with all the basic regulations so that you do not run into any legal issues later.

Wages and hours

It is very important to ensure that the wages are paid on time and that they are according to the laws of the state. It is also important to ensure that the employee hours are recorded accurately.

If you have a deadline approaching or a major business opportunity coming up, then it is very easy for you to slip up in this respect, and this could lead to legal issues later on. It is very important for HR personnel to keep a proper record of all these matters so that they can prove their case if need be. Also, never discriminate against any employee based on his/her religion, ethnicity, or gender. If you are found guilty of doing so, then it might lead to legal problems later.

As we have seen in this chapter, there are several legal issues faced by HR personnel which need special attention throughout their careers as human resource managers. While it is impossible for us to cover all these issues in detail here, there are certain basic things we have learned about how HR personnel can handle them as well as avoid them altogether. We have also seen how HR personnel can properly document all their activities and ensure they do not fall into any legal entanglements later.

Compliance with laws and regulations

The risk of legal action can be reduced by following laws and regulations in the company. The laws can be of local or national jurisdiction, but HR managers should make sure they are always adhering to them. In this case, the managers must create policies that are in accordance with the legal requirements and help their companies follow them.

There are several laws and regulations that human resource managers can come across in their work. Some of these include:

Discrimination laws, which prevent companies from discriminating against people on the basis of gender, race, nationality or age.

Equal Employment Opportunity (EEO) laws that prevent discrimination in favor or against a person based on their gender, race, or ethnicity.

Age discrimination which prevents employers from making any unfair decisions regarding employment due to their age.

Employment at will doctrine under which an employer has the right to terminate an employee without giving any reason why he/she is doing it.

This applies unless there is a contract between employer and employee to work for a certain time period or unless there is a special agreement between them for a specific period of time (called 'employment for definite period').

This provision also applies if the employee has been hired for a specific task, but the employer can terminate the employee any time before the deadline.

Employment discrimination

This refers to discrimination against an employee based on his/her race, gender, ethnicity, religion, and other things.

There are two major types of employment discrimination that human resource managers can come across:

Direct Discrimination

Discrimination by the employer based on his/her own prejudices (known as 'direct discrimination'). This is when a company discriminates against employees because of their race or religion.

For example, your company may not want any Muslim employees in it because of a certain religious belief of yours. This type of discrimination is unlawful and can be subject to legal action under the laws mentioned above.

Indirect Discrimination

Prejudice by other employers based on hiring practices (known as 'indirect discrimination'). Under this type of discrimination, your company will hire people not because they are capable employees but because they belong to a certain community or have a certain lifestyle that you like.

This type of indirect discrimination is also unlawful and can lead to legal action against your company if someone reports it.

There are several forms of discrimination which falls under diverse categories:

Direct and Indirect

Direct age discrimination is when an employer makes any decision based on the employee's age, for example when he/she refuses to hire someone because of his/her age. Indirect is when an employer only considers the employee's age while deciding about another factor unrelated to it. For example, when an employer decides on the basis of an applicant's experience and skill rather than considering his/her age as well.

Criminal Record Discrimination

In this type of discrimination, employers cannot use a person's criminal record against them while making decisions regarding their employment (such as hiring or promotion). Employers can ask for evidence about the person's criminal record if they suspect that they have committed any crime in their past but can only take it into consideration while making a final decision after considering other factors.

Sexual Discrimination

In this type of discrimination, companies cannot make any decision based on an employee's gender or sexual orientation. This means that an employer cannot discriminate against a female employee because he/she is of a different gender or sexual orientation.

Religious Discrimination

Human resource managers can also come across this type of employment law issue in which companies cannot make any decision based on the religion or religious views of their employees. This means that employers can't ask about the religion of their prospective employees during interviews or can't ask them to take their religious holidays off if it clashes with their work schedule.

Age Discrimination in Employment Act

Under this act, employees who are above 40 years old are not supposed to be terminated from their jobs unless they have violated some company policies and rules.

The only exception is if there is a financial crisis, and the company finds it necessary to let go of all of its employees to save itself from bankruptcy. In such cases, they will have to terminate all their employees irrespective of their age and not just those over 40 years old.

Under this type of employment law issue, companies cannot make any decision regarding employment based on the employee's age. All decisions, including hiring or firing employees, must be made based on a merit-based system. This means that no employee should be hired or fired just because he/she is above or below a certain age limit.

Americans with Disabilities Act

This act prohibits employers from terminating employees or harassing them because of their disabilities as well. An employee is considered to have a disability if he/she has a mental or physical impairment that makes performing his/her job difficult for him.

For example, if the person has lost one hand and needs an artificial hand to do his job, it can be seen as a disability as he cannot perform his work as efficiently without it.

The act also requires employers to make reasonable accommodations for employees with disabilities, so they can continue working without any issues.

Examples of reasonable accommodation include: allowing an employee to use a wheelchair if he/she is physically disabled, providing an interpreter for an employee who cannot speak English properly, or creating special workstations for employees who are visually impaired.

Equal Employment Opportunity Act

This act prevents discrimination in hiring practices based on gender, race, ethnicity, and other factors. Employers cannot take these factors into account when making decisions regarding hiring or firing employees unless there are legitimate reasons for doing so based on the nature of the job itself.

For example, if the job requires a person to work in a high-risk environment where he/she may get injured, it can be seen as a legitimate reason for not hiring women. In this case, the employer can feel inclined to hire men for the job, which also accounts as discrimination against women.

Employment terminations and layoffs

Employment terminations and layoffs are a very common issue. These occur when the organization feels that it cannot afford to keep a particular employee in its workforce. In the case of terminations, the employee is given proper notice, but in the case of layoffs, employees are not provided any notice.

The decision to terminate or lay off an employee is taken by the management of the organization. The decision should be backed by solid facts as well as evidence.

Both terminations and layoffs have some legal implications:

Terminations

Employment can be terminated either with or without cause and with or without notice. If you want to terminate someone's employment, you must follow certain principles laid down by law as well as the rules of your company. Let's look at them in detail:

To terminate an employee, you must follow proper due process and give ample amount of time for them to prove themselves if they are facing this termination for cause. This is called "probationary period" in layman's terms. During this period, both you and the employee will evaluate each other and see how they fit into their new roles.

Layoffs

The second type of termination is a layoff situation. This occurs when an organization needs to reduce its workforce to streamline its operations. The law does not mandate that you give notice or severance payments in case of layoffs either:

In case of layoffs, you only need to provide an adequate notice period so that employees can move on with their life and search for new jobs before they are laid off from your company. However, if you do decide to provide severance pay and/or other benefits along with the layoff package, it will be considered illegal and may result in several legal issues for your company; If you do provide severance pay and other benefits for layoff, you must ensure that these are given on an ad-hoc basis and not as a policy of your company.

Severance Pay

Severance pay is the amount of money that an employer is required to pay to the employee if they are terminated either with or without cause. This is to ensure that the employee gets a reasonable amount of money even if he or she is terminated from work.

In some cases, severance payments can be made in lieu of other benefits. For instance, in the case of you terminating someone's employment but at the same time providing them a retirement package, you don't have to give them any severance payments. The law does not mandate any specific payment for terminations without cause. However, there is a common practice where employers give employees some amount of money which is called "severance pay" in layman's terms.

If you decide to do this, make sure that you give it only on an ad-hoc basis and not as a policy of your company. You should also ensure that the decision to give this payment is taken on a case-to-case basis and not as a blanket offer across all employees. If you have a policy of giving severance pay to employees who are let go, you must make sure that this is not discriminatory.

For instance, if you are giving this to all of the employees who work in the Marketing department but not to any of the employees who work in the Sales department, it will be considered discriminatory. If any employee is terminated for a cause and they do not get any severance pay, they can file for unemployment benefits. If you terminate someone's employment without cause, or if you give them less than required notice period, then they can file for unemployment benefits as well.

Hiring employees

In a company, hiring employees is a major task. It may be the first thing you do when you start working and the last thing you do before going home. There are many legal issues that can crop up in this process. Things like discrimination, back-dating of contracts and fraud can all come up.

Here are some ways to ensure the legality of your hiring procedures:

Advertise for the job properly

In most cases, it is illegal to advertise for a job if it's already filled by someone else, if there is already an internal candidate working for that position or if there's no vacancy at all. In such cases, you need to be very careful about how you advertise for the post. You must mention in your advertisement that this is only an opening for internal candidates and that there are no external candidates interested in this position at present. You must also mention how long you're going to keep this post vacant (for example: 6 months) so as not to attract any external candidates who don't know about the vacancy. Of course, making a false claim like saying nobody wants this job will land you in trouble as well.

The standard way to advertise an opening is to say that this is an opening for a certain type of person, and that you will interview candidates in your office. Finally, you should mention in the ad that any external candidate will have to go through the same process as any internal candidate.

Equal opportunity

As per the laws, it's illegal to hire only people of a particular gender and age group or those who belong to a particular religion or caste. You need to make sure that your company doesn't discriminate against anyone on these grounds. If you hire someone who is not qualified, it would also be illegal as they are not eligible for the job. So, make sure you don't do any of these things, especially when it comes to government jobs where there are many rules regarding this aspect of hiring people.

Hiring illegal immigrants

If you hire a person who does not have the legal right to be in the country, then you will face legal problems. So, it goes without saying that you should only hire people who are legally allowed to work in the country. You also need to be very careful when hiring foreign nationals as they might not have the necessary documents and might not be qualified for the job.

Discrimination

As mentioned above, you cannot discriminate against any potential candidate on account of their gender, age, or religion. So, make sure that you follow this rule strictly when hiring people. If you don't do so, your company will face all sorts of legal problems and may even be shut down if such discrimination is proven to be widespread in your company.

Overtime payments

It is illegal for your company to force employees to work overtime or make them do it against their will. In such cases, the employee can sue your company for all sorts of damages and can even get punitive damages if he or she has suffered mental trauma. So, make sure that employers are given a choice before being asked to work overtime, and make sure they are compensated adequately if they choose to do so under duress.

Contracts

When you hire a new employee, you must give them a contract which clearly states the terms and conditions of their employment. It is illegal for you to alter this contract without the consent of the employee or to omit any of its terms without informing the employee. If you do so, then your company will face legal problems. It's also illegal for you to hold back or withhold an employee's salary or pay them in cash instead of depositing it into their bank account. Also, if an employee resigns from your company, he or she must be given all the benefits specified in their employment contract within 10 working days. If they are not paid on time, then they can sue your company for all sorts of damages, and may even get punitive damages if they have suffered mental trauma due to delayed payment. So, make sure that you follow these rules strictly when dealing with employees, otherwise your company will face legal troubles from time to time.

These are just a few of the legal issues that you will face when you hire new employees. There are several other legal issues that you might encounter in your career as an HR manager.

Chapter 7: HR Systems and Technology

An organization's ability to deliver quality products and services is directly linked to its ability to manage its workforce. Strategic planning and managing employee performance are critical components of any organization's success in today's ever-changing business environment. The need for maintaining competitive pricing structures to stay in business requires companies to focus on reducing their cost of operations, driving efficiencies, improving productivity, and streamlining their operations. This is where the Human Resources function comes into the picture.

This is where HR systems and technology are critical. The role of the Human Resources function is to manage and administer various functions that support the organization's human resources goals and objectives. HR systems support most of these functions and therefore are critical in performing an organization's Human Resources activities.

The HR systems and technology are rapidly changing as we enter the e-business era. To keep pace with these changes, businesses need to look at their existing HR systems and technologies, recognize their strengths, weaknesses, opportunities, and threats (SOWTs), along with issues and challenges and plan accordingly for the future. Technology can provide business organizations with significant benefits that can increase productivity, lower operating costs, improve efficiency and increase earnings by providing a competitive advantage. However, these advantages can only be achieved if the business organization takes a proactive approach towards identifying its needs prior to implementing a new technology solution or upgrading their current technology solution.

This chapter will look at some of the challenges businesses face when implementing or upgrading their Human Resource Systems (HR Systems). This chapter will also introduce some of the latest technologies and best practices that businesses can use to address these challenges. A good understanding of these issues will enable business organizations to plan and implement effective HR Systems to effectively manage their workforce.

Achieving Results through Human Resource Systems

Business organizations have many different systems in place to manage their operations and achieve results. Most of these systems are aligned with the business organization's strategies, objectives and goals and are designed to help the business organization achieve these goals. The Human Resource (HR) department is no different; it too has various systems in place to support its operations. These systems are designed to help the HR department achieve its strategic objectives and goals.

For the HR department to achieve its strategic objectives, it needs to have the right systems in place. A good HR system is one that is designed to meet the needs of the organization as well as support the HR department's mission and strategic objectives. This means that the HR systems need to be aligned with the organization's overall strategies, have a robust functional set with integrated capabilities, be flexible enough to change with business requirements and be able to support future business growth. However, in today's business environment, it is important for businesses to focus on using technology as a competitive advantage. Technology is critical in helping businesses achieve their strategic goals and objectives, and businesses need new ways of thinking about how they can use technology to achieve these results.

The importance of implementing an integrated HR system cannot be over emphasized. Such a system will give organizations significant advantages in terms of improving effectiveness of managing their workforce, enhancing productivity, reducing operating costs and driving efficiencies.

Challenges Faced by Organizations

Implementing or upgrading an existing HR system is not an easy task. There are many things to consider when making this decision or implementing and upgrading. In this section, we will look at some of the challenges that organizations face when implementing or upgrading their HR systems.

First, it is important to understand what comprises an HR system and how it is meant to be used. An HR system is a set of technologies, processes and tools designed to support the management of human resources in an organization. The function of this system is to support the strategic objectives of the business organization by ensuring that it has a quality workforce that can help achieve its strategic objectives.

The HR system usually consists of several components that work together to provide a complete suite of HR services for the management and development of employees. This means that each component must have direct links with other components or elements within the system so as to create a cohesive set of processes and/or tools that can effectively be used by managers and employees alike (e.g., hiring process and performance appraisal processes).

When designing an HR system, it is important for organizations to carefully consider their current business environment as well as future objectives and goals. The functions and features offered by each component should be aligned with these requirements to ensure efficiency and effectiveness in achieving results and managing human resources. The future business environment could have an impact on the HR system; for example, a business organization that is considering expanding its operations internationally may need to consider adding an international HR component to its existing HR system.

Deciding on a Technology Vendor

One of the biggest challenges that organizations face when implementing or upgrading their HR system is deciding on a vendor or vendor set. This decision can be made based on different criteria, such as expertise in HR systems, cost, and ability to deliver. However, it is important to understand that there are several issues associated with selecting a vendor or a set of vendors for your organization's HR system.

For example, if your organization's current systems are not performing effectively and you decide to upgrade your old systems, there could be some challenges in transferring data from your old systems to the new ones.

To avoid this problem, it would be advisable for organizations to first get help from their IT department when designing their new systems so that they can make provisions for data transfer procedures as well as assist in choosing the right vendors.

Required Components for the HR System

Another big challenge faced by organizations is deciding which components need to be included in their new HR system and the level at which these components need to perform at. This means that organizations must first identify what they want each component to offer and then find out which vendors can offer those features.

This could be a challenge because there are several HR vendors in the market, and each vendor may have a different way of looking at HR systems and the way they should perform. This means that organizations will have to determine which vendor or set of vendors can best provide the features required for their HR system.

Upgrading or Migrating

Another issue that organizations face when implementing or upgrading their HR systems is determining whether they need to implement a totally new system or whether they should upgrade their existing systems.

The decision to upgrade current systems rather than implement a completely new one could be because organizations do not want to have any downtime while implementing a new system as well as the cost associated with implementing a completely new system.

However, it is important for organizations to understand that when upgrading existing systems, it is not easy to incorporate future business requirements into existing systems as opposed to implementing a new one where it would be relatively easy to add functionality by simply installing additional modules for an appropriate price.

Number of Vendors to Use

It can also be challenging for organizations to decide on how many vendors will be used in their HR System; this means that you must decide whether you will use one single company for all your HR needs or use different vendors for different HR functions. The decision to use different vendors for different HR functions has many benefits such as greater flexibility, better pricing, and better integration among modules. This may be a challenge because it could be more difficult to manage the design and implementation of the entire HR system by using several vendors.

Having the Right Technical Talents for Maintenance

Another challenge organizations face when implementing or upgrading their HR systems is putting together the right team of people who can develop and implement the necessary strategies that will help them meet their goals and objectives. This means that organizations should have individuals with sufficient expertise in both HR management as well as information technology to get this right.

It is important for organizations to understand that they need to have individuals with appropriate knowledge of both fields so that they can effectively design, implement and manage their new systems; however, it is also important not to lose sight of the purpose of implementing an HR system to achieve strategic objectives.

When implementing or upgrading an existing system, it is important for organizations to make sure that they do not overlook any essential components when designing their new system; this means that they must ensure that each component supports business requirements as well as provide effective user interfaces (UI).

If certain components are not included in your new system, then you may not be able to achieve your strategic objectives or fulfill any legal requirements. It is also important for organizations to consider the impact of each component on the cost of implementing a new system; this means that organizations should try and minimize cost while still ensuring that they get all the different components that are needed for their HR system.

Now that we have seen some of the challenges organizations face when implementing or upgrading their HR systems, we will now introduce the HR systems in a sequence that would best align with the normal ways that HR activities are performed.

Employee Relations Management Systems

Employee Relations Management Systems are used by organizations to manage the relationship between the organization and its employees. While the existence of

Employee Relations Management Systems is generally acknowledged, there is little consensus on their purpose, form, or function. It is acknowledged that there is a need to balance efficiency and effectiveness to maintain a sustainable and effective Employee Relations Management System.

Employee relations are mostly defined in terms of the goals of the organization. There are several broad categories of employee relations goals:

The most common goal is to create strong employee relations through the development of a positive relationship between the employee and the organization. The relationship is considered positive if there is mutual trust, respect, and support. It is also important that employees be involved in decisions that affect their jobs.

The second most common goal is to ensure efficient and effective operation of the organization through such mechanisms as performance management, training, communications, grievance handling, employment contracts and discipline process.

The third most common goal is to ensure legal compliance. This is done through the creation of policies and procedures as well as through human resource information systems that store employment data.

Employee Relations Management Systems are complex and multifaceted and can be viewed from many different perspectives. The three most common perspectives are: job analysis, organizational analysis, and human resource management.

Typical technology components of Employee Relations Management Systems include:

Employee Records

Employee records are the foundation of any Employee Relations Management System. They are the primary source of information for development of employment related policies and procedures, job analysis and performance management. An effective Employee Relations Management System ensures that these records are kept up to date, accurate and secure.

For example, Human Resources Management Systems typically include a personnel database. The database contains employee information such as contact information, employment dates, job descriptions and performance appraisal ratings.

Employee Records Management

Employee records are often stored in files that are managed by an employee records manager or human resources manager. Records managers keep records up to date, ensure compliance with legislation and policies, and in some cases handle the retention of the records.

Employee Benefits

Employee benefit plans are an integral part of an organization's Employee Relations Management System. These plans include such things as pension, health insurance and bonuses. They are generally governed by government legislation and are typically administered by a benefits manager or Human Resources manager.

Performance Management

Employee performance is generally measured by how well employees accomplish their assigned tasks or duties. Performance is usually tracked through such mechanisms as job analysis, performance measurement and performance appraisal systems. These systems are typically managed by a human resources manager or performance management specialist.

For example, a performance management system might measure the number of hours each day that an employee is at work on the job, the number of correct answers on a test or quiz and then provide a score based on that measurement.

Training and Development

Training and development are important activities in any Employee Relations Management System. Training and development activities can be used to improve individual performance and organizational effectiveness through such mechanisms as formal training programs, job rotation programs, mentoring programs, and knowledge management systems. These activities are typically managed by a training/development manager or human resources manager.

For example, a knowledge management system could be used to create databases containing information on specific projects, products, services, or procedures that would be available for employees to consult when needed.

Human Resource Information Systems

Human Resource Information Systems (HRIS) are electronic information systems that manage human resource activities such as recruitment, payroll, benefits, performance evaluation, and employee self-service. Human Resource Information Systems have evolved from the human resource information management systems of the 1970s and 1980s. Today's HRIS are often part of larger Enterprise Resource Planning (ERP) systems that manage all business operations.

Human Resource Information Systems are a subsystem of Enterprise Applications, which is a common term for software used to automate business processes. Other subsystems include Financial Applications, Customer Relationship Management (CRM), Sales Force Automation (SFA), Supply Chain Management (SCM) and Business Intelligence and Analytics.

What Does the Human Resource Information System Do?

The Human Resource Information System (HRIS) is an information system that, in real time, manages and stores all a company's human resource information. The HRIS automates human resource activities such as hiring employees, processing payroll, managing benefits, managing employee performance and appraisals, providing online training and development and other functions.

What is the Role of an HRIS?

The main role of an HRIS is to automate human resource activities. The most important function of the HRIS is the management and storage of employee data such as employee personnel files. An HRIS manages all company-related information about employees who work for a business. As such, it provides a central database that employees can use to access their own personnel information. The system helps the company manage its workforce by providing multiple layers of access controls to protect employee data from unauthorized access.

The main features of an HRIS are:

Recruitment, hiring, and employment.

This module of an HRIS automates activities related to recruiting and hiring new employees. The system can be used to generate job descriptions, post job openings, screen candidates via job interviews, send automated job offers and rejections to candidates, process employee background checks and employment applications and perform other vital functions.

Payroll Processing

The payroll module of an HRIS handles all employee payroll-related tasks. These include the evaluation of employees' pay rates based on their performance or seniority level and calculation of their salary deductions such as taxes, retirement contributions and health insurance premiums. The system typically also manages pay slips, and tax forms such as W2s and 1099s.

Budgeting & Financial Management

The financial management module of an HRIS is responsible for taking real-time information about the company's financial data (such as employee salaries) and building financial models that assist business decision-making processes such as budgeting for future expenses. This module also calculates taxes based on employees' salary deductions. Additionally, this module manages the company's financial forecasting process by taking input from various business functions such as sales forecasts from vendors or customers. It creates financial reports for management or external stakeholders that detail the company's financial health.

Benefits Administration

The benefits administration module of an HRIS manages the company's employee benefits packages. This includes tracking the amount of paid versus accrued vacation time and calculating the amount of holiday pay that an employee will receive based on their hourly earnings. Other tasks include tracking annual holidays and sick days for employees and calculating and paying out bonuses based on performance or seniority. The system is often integrated with a third-party benefits vendor to handle the administration of employee benefits such as health insurance or 401Ks.

Performance Management & Appraisals

The performance management module of an HRIS tracks employee performance records such as attendance records, number of projects completed and salary or bonus adjustments. It also tracks employee training programs with automated reports on how much an employee has learned through a given training program. In addition to recording training information, this module manages performance reviews with automated reminders to managers about upcoming reviews and reports summarizing an employee's performance during a given time period (usually a quarter). This module also allows employees to prepare for reviews by updating their personnel files, requesting additional documentation from their managers about poor evaluations and other employee information. Managers use these features to write and submit performance evaluations for each of their employees.

Employee Self-Service

The employee self-service module of an HRIS allows employees to access their personnel records, check their pay rates, request time off and other self-service functions. This module also helps manage the company's employee benefits by allowing employees to adjust the amount of their personal contributions toward health insurance premiums or retirement plan contributions. Employees can also use this module to file for medical leaves or vacations. The system will automatically determine if an employee is entitled to a vacation or sick day based on his/her past record, then approve the request and send out a notification email when it's approved.

HR Management & Administration

The HR management and administration module of an HRIS is responsible for managing all human resource-related activities including changes in personnel policies, new hiring decisions (such as the addition of new employees), employee terminations and other crucial functions. This module also handles tax reporting (such as 1099s) and tax deductions (such as payroll taxes). It is usually integrated with a third-party tax filing services provider or with a General Ledger system to calculate these tax amounts. Additionally, this module tracks employee performance evaluations such as attendance and other performance metrics.

Human Resources Metrics & Analytics

The human resources analytics module of an HRIS is responsible for generating reports and charts that summarize the company's HR information. These reports can be used to monitor the number of employees who are eligible for retirement, or to track the number of new hires in a given time period. The system can also be used to track employee turnover rates and the number of hours employees have worked. This information can be used by managers and executives to track compliance with company policies, predict future personnel expenses, and make strategic decisions about hiring new employees. This module is usually integrated with a third-party data analytics service such as Google Analytics or Adobe Analytics.

Application Tracking System

The application tracking system is a database that contains all the information related to the applicants and their applications. It stores personal information (such as name, address, contact number, education details and experience) as well as official data (such as application date, status, status changes, comments, and other relevant information). The applicant tracking system makes it easier for the recruiter to keep track of applicant history and communicate with them.

When an employee or a candidate applies for a job, they will be asked to submit their personal details on an application form. This data is then stored in an applicant tracking system. The application tracking system helps recruiters to store all the information about candidates who have applied for jobs in their company and to also keep track of who has applied for what job. Application tracking systems are built with advanced search features that help find candidates based on certain criteria such as location or experience level.

The applicant tracking system is a great way for companies to get a bigger pool of candidates to choose from. It also helps the company to filter out candidates based on their skills and experience level.

The main features of an applicant tracking system are:

- Capturing application data
- Assessing and evaluating candidates
- Maintaining candidate information
- Personalizing communication with candidates
- Easily searching for candidates
- Keeping track of all application data
  This system helps recruiters to stay organized and do their job more efficiently

Benefits of an Applicant Tracking System

An applicant tracking system is a one stop shop for all job application related data such as resumes, application forms, interview notes and performance reviews. It makes it easier for recruiters to re-use the data rather than having to enter the same information again and again. This helps in a faster hiring process.

Recruiters can create custom views of candidates based on their skillset, experience level, location, or other criteria. This helps recruiters find ideal candidates quickly and easily without having to go through hundreds of resumes or applications.

Benefits for the Candidate

Applicant tracking systems make it easier for candidates to track their application status and communicate with recruiters. They can also add or update their application information whenever they want through the system.

This system makes it easier for applicants to keep track of their applications and always know what is happening with it. It also helps applicants to communicate with recruiters easily and quickly.

Learning and Development Systems

These systems are the center for learning and development (L&D) in an organization. These systems typically include eLearning, training management, coaching and performance management systems. L&D systems typically provide a central location for organizing and facilitating learning and development activities within an organization (e.g., training, coaching and performance management).

In the Human Resources Management System, L&D systems may include:

LMS/CMS

Learning Management System/Content Management System - An online system that allows learners to access course content and instructor-led sessions. Web conferencing tools are also integrated into LMSs.

ALM

Applicant & Learning Management System - A learning management system used to manage applications for employees, interns, or contract positions. This system is often integrated with other applicant tracking systems listed below.

Learning Management Systems (LMS) is a term that has been adopted by various technology companies in the e-learning industry to describe their specific product offerings. The term was first coined by a company called OpenSesame in 1999 with the launch of their online training solution.

Since then, almost every major company in the e-learning space has come up with their own interpretation of what "Learning Management Systems" mean to them, leading to a lot of confusion in the marketplace as users try to determine which product will best suit their needs.
To make things more confusing, the term Learning Management System, or LMS, is also loosely used to describe online training delivery platforms (i.e., the software-as-a-service or SaaS model) that are used by several different companies.

The primary purpose of an LMS is to provide an infrastructure that enables organizations to create and manage training programs. It can be used for a variety of functions including creating courses and content, delivering programs through various methods (traditional classroom, e-learning, video, self-study), tracking and reporting on both learner progress and instructor performance, managing course enrollments and access rights.

The key feature of any LMS is its flexibility: it allows users to build a wide range of training solutions without having to start from scratch each time. The other major benefit is that it helps eliminate duplication of effort within an organization by centralizing all training information in one place.

An LMS provides an easy way for trainers to build courses and materials without having in-depth technical knowledge about web development languages like HTML5 or Flash. This enables them to focus more on their content creation skills rather than becoming experts in learning application development. It also makes it easier for them to share their content with others in their organization who may be better at developing courses for specific business functions.

A key component of any LMS is the course management features. At a minimum, an LMS should enable instructors to create and manage courses and content in an easy-to-use interface. It should also provide some basic reporting capabilities that help instructors track learner progress and understand how well the course is performing.

Some LMS systems take this concept a step forward by allowing instructors to customize the way they deliver training to different audiences through different delivery methods. This can be particularly useful when training must be delivered in multiple languages, or if it needs to be delivered over several different channels like traditional classroom, e-learning or video-based learning.

Another important feature of any LMS is its integrations with other enterprise software such as HR, learning management systems or employer branding portals. Integrations with these systems help ensure that employee records are always up-to-date and there are no duplicate entries across multiple applications.

For example, if an employee registers for an online course through their eLearning portal but has already completed it through their LMS, the information will instantly appear as a conflict in both applications and will prevent any further work being carried out until the conflict is resolved.

A great example will be Cudy LMS, one of the best LMS in the market. Cudy LMS is an online training platform that allows organizations to create courses and content, manage their learning programs and track their training metrics. As a cloud-based solution, it's easy to deploy and requires no additional hardware or software. Cudy LMS is a SaaS solution that can be easily integrated with other systems in your organization to ensure that you're always up-to-date with data from other systems such as HR, payroll or CRM systems.

Benefits of a L&D System

LMS helps employees to improve their knowledge and skills, thereby improving their career prospects and boosting productivity. It also helps in reducing employee turnover rates by adding new features that employees can use to enhance their skills.

It saves time for both the employer as well as the employee by automating the training process. Employees do not need to spend time registering in a training course or going to classes. They just log into their account and start learning anytime and anywhere on any platform they choose.

LMS also enables the employer to track the progress of each employee, which can be helpful in making better decisions regarding hiring, promotions, transfers or compensation of an employee. This is very useful when there are many employees operating at different geographical locations.

It is a cost-effective solution as it reduces travel cost and hence improves the operational efficiency of an organization. Employees can learn from any location with access to the internet at any time with a single login ID.

It allows organizations to control all training material through one interface which prevents information duplication, making it easy for managers and HR departments to track training metrics such as completion rates, enrollment numbers, other statistics and make important business decisions based on these metrics.

It utilizes content management system technology to enable organizations to store, track and distribute training content.

LMS also gives the employer freedom in terms of designing their own training program based on needs and available budgets. It helps them customize training for each employee depending upon their expertise and work experience.

Enterprise Communication System

Enterprise Communication Software is an umbrella term that refers to software that allows users of the software to communicate with each other in real-time. The software is used to facilitate communication between employees of a company and may be used to allow other companies or individuals to communicate with employees of a company.

Examples include an enterprise messaging system, enterprise social networking, enterprise collaboration and community building and enterprise crowdsourcing.

Enterprise Collaboration Software is a type of Enterprise Communication Software that allows for content creation by multiple users simultaneously using an interface. The content created can be shared and can be edited by multiple users simultaneously.

Examples include Enterprise Social Networking, Enterprise Crowdsourcing, Enterprise Social Analytics, and Content Management Systems (CMS).

Enterprise Social Analytics

Enterprise Social Analytics is a type of Enterprise Collaboration Software that allows for real-time analysis on the collaboration activities that are taking place. Social analytics can analyze the collaboration patterns of individuals as well as entire business units. Examples include Enterprise Social Networking Analytics, Enterprise Crowdsourcing Analytics, and LMS Analytics.

Enterprise Social Networking

Enterprise Social Networking is a type of Enterprise Collaboration Software that allows for the creation of social networks for individuals within a company, between companies in an industry, or between companies and their customers. Examples include Google+, Facebook Pages/Groups/Companies, Twitter Account/Profilers, LinkedIn Company Pages/Company Profiles, Quora Company Pages/Company Profiles and Yammer Groups.

Enterprise Crowdsourcing

Enterprise Collaboration Software is a type of Enterprise Communication Software that allows users to post tasks or problems on the software for other users to solve as part of a group effort. This can be done in real-time and usually utilizes an interface that allows for simultaneous input by multiple users. Examples include Evernote Spots/Ideas, Zoho Projects Ideas Board, Wrike Ideas Board, Flow Ideas Board, Asana Ideas Board and Trello Cards/Boards.

Conclusion

We have come to the end of the book Human Resources Essentials. We hope that you enjoyed reading this book as much as we enjoyed writing it.

"No one can whistle a symphony. It takes an orchestra to play it." - H.E. Luccock

While this book is designed to be a resource guide for HR managers and business owners, it is also a resource for those who are seeking to enter the world of Human Resources. It is our hope that this book has provided you with a solid foundation in the world of HR and given you the tools to succeed in this field.

As you have now seen, there is much more to Human Resources than just recruiting or dealing with employee issues. It is an in-depth profession that requires years of study and practice before one can be considered an expert in the field.

Managing employees efficiently and effectively requires a considerable amount of time, effort, and resources. Since employees are the most valuable assets of a company, it is necessary that they are managed well to ensure the productivity of the company.

This book has provided a comprehensive understanding of how to deal with the various aspects of employee management and HR planning. The book has covered the following:

- The importance of employee management
- The challenges of effective employee management
- Managing employees in difficult situations
- Planning and implementing employee training programs
- Incorporating human resources processes into business functions
- Utilizing employee surveys for better management
- Implementing workplace policies for effective employee management
- Managing employee compensation effectively
- Managing employee benefits effectively

Overall, this book has stressed the importance of effective and efficient employee management and how it can be achieved in a company through a variety of means.

That being said, we hope that you will continue to use this book as a resource for years to come, and may even refer back to it from time to time as questions arise.

We hope that this book has provided valuable information that will assist many businesses in managing their employees effectively and efficiently.

Good luck in your future career!

www.ingramcontent.com/pod-product-compliance
Lightning Source LLC
LaVergne TN
LVHW010259260326
834688LV00044B/1371